P9-AOB-094

Crisis intervention as psychotherapy

Robert J Baxter

Pauline L. Rabin

Crisis intervention as psychotherapy

CHARLES PATRICK EWING

Coordinator of Children's Services
Genesee Mental Health Center
Rochester, New York

New York   OXFORD UNIVERSITY PRESS   1978

Copyright © 1978 by Oxford University Press, Inc.

Library of Congress Cataloging in Publication Data

Ewing, Charles Patrick, 1949-
Crisis intervention as psychotherapy.

Bibliography: p.
Includes index.
1. Crisis intervention (Psychiatry) I. Title.
[DNLM: 1. Crisis intervention. 2. Psychotherapy. WM420 E95c]
RC480.6.E93   616.8′914   77-13127
ISBN 0-19-502270-X
ISBN 0-19-502271-8 pbk.

VANDERBILT UNIVERSITY
MEDICAL CENTER LIBRARY

JUL 28 1986

NASHVILLE, TENNESSEE
37232

Printed in the United States of America

Preface

I was introduced to crisis intervention in the Spring of 1973 by Dr. Leon O. Brenner and Patricia Ewalt of the Framingham Youth Guidance Center in Framingham, Massachusetts. Their "Crisis Clinic," which is described in Chapter 5 of this volume, was utilizing crisis intervention as a form of psychotherapy for children and their families. I was excited by what I learned of the "Crisis Clinic" approach and decided to devote my doctoral research to a study of its efficacy. My clinical experience and research at the Youth Guidance Center convinced me that crisis intervention was a widely applicable, often effective, yet relatively inexpensive form of psychotherapy.

I should make it clear from the outset that I am an enthusiastic proponent of crisis intervention as psychotherapy. As a psychotherapist, I have found it useful with a wide variety of clients. As a researcher, I have begun to develop empirical evidence that it is at least as effective as other more traditional psychotherapies—if not more effective. As a clinical administrator, I see crisis intervention as an important means of extending limited clinical resources to make services available to an ever-growing client population.

As an author, however, I have tried to curb my enthusiasm and bias in an effort to present a dispassionate, critical account of the theory, practice, and evaluation of crisis intervention as psychotherapy. I have been assisted greatly in this effort by colleagues in various mental health professions who have reviewed the manuscript and offered useful criticisms and suggestions. Marcus Boggs of Oxford University Press has also been helpful in many ways, especially in suggesting the inclusion of a clinical model useful to beginning-level psychotherapists.

Finally, and most importantly, I must acknowledge the major role played in the development of this book by my wife, Sharon Harris-Ewing, who has been both my greatest supporter and severest critic. Her editorial and substantive contributions have been invaluable. I am delighted to dedicate this work to her.

New Haven, Connecticut   C. P. E.
March, 1977

Contents

Crisis intervention as psychotherapy

I

1

Introduction

The "crisis" in crisis intervention

Over the past decade or so, the term "crisis intervention" has steadily crept into the working vocabulary of most mental health professionals as well as that of many social scientists. Despite (or perhaps because of) its increasing currency, the term seems in recent years to have become shrouded in confusion, if not controversy. One is tempted to say that the concept itself is in a state of "crisis."

Social scientists speak of crisis intervention as a conceptual model for understanding human adjustment, family dynamics, and even organizational development. Community mental health workers view it variously as a strategy for the prevention of mental disorder and psychiatric hospitalization, a form of short-term psychotherapy, a model for community consultation, and as a rationale for new self-help and paraprofessional programs. Finally, some journalists have gone so far as to hail crisis intervention as the third great revolution in the field of mental health.

Even among professionals approaching crisis intervention with similar goals or intentions, there remains much confusion and controversy over what the concept means. For example, in a given community, the adult mental health clinic may offer walk-in counseling services, the child development council may provide stimulating day-care services for the underprivileged, the social services department may offer temporary "homemakers" to families with disruptive difficulties such as hospitalization of a parent, the local suicide prevention society may sponsor a 24-hour telephone "hotline," the child guidance center may provide short-term intensive family therapy on a no-wait basis, and the local police force may have been trained to use psychological techniques to calm the disputants in domestic disturbance calls. All these community helpers offer something quite different to the respective "clienteles," and yet each may well claim to be "doing" crisis intervention.

—Or, as has actually happened in the author's experience, the faculty of an academic department of psychology may meet to consider a proposed course on "crisis intervention," only to discover that each member of the department has his own ideas as to what should and should not be included in the curriculum.

So, despite or perhaps because of its wide acceptance as an approach to a gamut of concerns about human behavior, crisis intervention seems to have evolved as a rather vague, poorly defined, and ill-articulated concept, used by many but understood by probably only a few.

Were mere semantics the issue, then perhaps this state of confusion could be allowed to stand indefinitely, with definitional license granted to anyone with good intentions. Unfortunately, however, the problems associated with this confusion go well beyond so simplistic a concern for specificity of words. The proliferation of models, courses, activities, techniques, and programs self-described (and at times self-justified) as being grounded in the principles of crisis intervention should give pause to all who are concerned with the study and/or modification of human behavior. Whether scientists, clinicians, students, or simply concerned laymen, we have the right, if not the responsibility, to question the basis, rationale, meaning, and usefulness of any concept purporting to explain or modify any aspect of human behavior. With a concept such as crisis intervention, which shows signs of becoming a fad or "bandwagon" movement, an intelligent questioning of this sort appears no less than imperative.

It is with this conviction, born of a concern for those who would understand and modify behavior as well as for those who would seek to have their behavior understood and modified, that the present volume is intended to question in these very ways some of the principles and practices that have come to be known as crisis intervention.

In an effort to clarify rather than obscure further the meaning of this popular concept, this volume addresses itself to only one of the many contexts in which crisis intervention is currently used—the psychotherapeutic relationship. Thus, while not denying its validity or usefulness in other contexts, this work represents an attempt to provide a broad and clear, yet concise and critical review of crisis intervention as it is currently used as a form of psychotherapy.

Crisis intervention as psychotherapy: Why?

The decision to so limit the scope of this work appears warranted by a number of considerations. First of all, a thorough and fair review of the entire field of crisis intervention would be well beyond the scope of even the most ambitious volumes. For those seeking a far-ranging (though by no means thorough) review of the field as a whole, several collections of useful, if diverse, readings are available elsewhere (e.g., Parad, 1965; Specter and Claiborn, 1973).

Of even greater practical import, however, is the clear observation that by far the most popular use of crisis intervention is as a form of psychotherapy. Despite the multitude of uses to which its techniques are being put, even the most cursory review of the literature of psychology, social work, nursing, and psychiatry provides abundant evidence that crisis intervention is most often understood and used as psychotherapy. Running a popular but still distant second to psychotherapy is the use of these techniques in community suicide prevention. McGee (1974) and Lester and Brockoff (1973) provide excellent descriptions of recent advances in this area.

Finally, it should be noted that perhaps crisis intervention is most clearly understandable as a form of psychotherapy because the theory upon which it is based has evolved largely out of the psychotherapeutic experiences of a group of practicing clinicians (e.g., Lindemann, 1944; Caplan, 1964; Rapoport, 1962). In general, the leading theorists in crisis intervention have not limited their formulations to the psychotherapeutic. And yet, as will be seen in the chapters to follow, they and their colleagues and followers have most often found in crisis theory the basis for principles and techniques clearly designed for psychotherapeutic use.

Crisis intervention as psychotherapy: What?

Some no doubt would argue, more or less convincingly, that nearly all uses of crisis intervention are psychotherapeutic—or at least intended to be so. The question of what is and is not psychotherapeutic has long plagued mental health professionals, particularly those interested in evaluating methods of behavior change. While it is unlikely that any one definition of psychotherapy, for example, will ever find universal acceptance, it is incumbent upon those of us who write of this phenomenon to define our terms. When considering a specialized form of psychotherapy such as crisis intervention—already shrouded in confusion—the need for clear definition is even more urgent. With this in view, the present author has chosen to define crisis intervention by paraphrasing the popular definition of psychotherapy of Meltzoff and Kornreich (1970). For present purposes, then, crisis intervention is *the informed and planful application of techniques derived from the established principles of crisis theory, by persons qualified through training and experience to understand these principles, with the intention of assisting individuals or families to modify personal characteristics such as feelings, attitudes, and behaviors that are judged to be maladaptive or maladjustive.*

While this definition is somewhat general, by intent it excludes many helping efforts heretofore designated as crisis intervention. The intent here is not to judge these other efforts as less valuable or meaningful, but rather only to delineate carefully the scope of the present work. For instance, while there is no doubt that all sorts of relationships may be beneficial to the individual or family in crisis, the terms "informed and planful" adopted here rule out informal or casual contacts with others which may prove therapeutic. As it is conceived here, crisis intervention involves a relatively structured and planned encounter between client and therapist in which both are aware of and agreed upon the therapeutic nature and aims of their relationship.

Moreover, the phrase "derived from the established principles of crisis theory" precludes consideration of other relationships or services which, though helpful, cannot legitimately be tied to the theoretical foundations of crisis intervention. This aspect of the definition, however, in no way precludes consideration of the use of external relationships or services within the context of crisis intervention as psychotherapy. As will be emphasized throughout this volume, crisis therapists frequently make use of the client's important relationships as well as other resources available to the client in the community.

Finally, and perhaps most importantly—given the current trend in community mental-health services—the phrase "qualified through training and experience" eliminates consideration of the increasingly large number of services being offered by untrained or minimally trained nonprofessional volunteers or employees. While relatively untrained laymen may make significant contributions to community mental health programs, the emphasis of the present work is on the use of crisis intervention by trained, professional psychotherapists. Useful descriptions of the contribution of lay volunteers and paraprofessionals to crisis intervention programs are available elsewhere (Helig, Farberow, Litman and Schneidman, 1968; Lester and Brockoff, 1973; Specter and Claiborn, 1973). The question of lay *versus* professional crisis intervention has been touched upon by McColskey (1973) and will be considered briefly in Chapter 8 of the present volume.

The above definition of crisis intervention should be kept in mind by the reader, since it has served as the principle for selection of most of the material reviewed in the ensuing chapters. Still, crisis intervention, like any other psychotherapy, is perhaps defined most meaningfully by the ways in which it is utilized. It is hoped that the chapters to follow will provide the reader with a both practical and professionally useful account of the contemporary meaning of crisis intervention as psychotherapy.

Crisis intervention as psychotherapy: Plan of the book

To this end, this volume was planned in two sections, the first to contain the following:

A systematic presentation of the basics of crisis intervention theory as it has evolved over the past three decades or more (Chapter 2);

A statement of what appear to be general principles in the current use of crisis intervention as psychotherapy (Chapter 3);

A broad review of current psychotherapeutic uses of crisis intervention (Chapter 4);

A detailed look at several apparently successful crisis-therapy programs (Chapter 5);

A critical review of the evaluative research done to date on crisis intervention as psychotherapy (Chapter 6);

Specific suggestions regarding the appropriateness of crisis intervention for various client populations, derived from researches of the present author and others (Chapter 7);

Some observations regarding the future of crisis intervention practice and research (Chapter 8).

This material is followed by a second section offering a model for the clinical practice of crisis intervention as psychotherapy. It is hoped that this model will be useful particularly to the novice therapist with little or no experience in crisis intervention.

2

The theoretical base

Crisis theory—the basis for most current programs of crisis intervention—has evolved largely through the work of Erich Lindemann, Gerald Caplan, their students, colleagues, and followers. As was noted earlier, this theory has its roots in the clinical experience of these practicing professionals.

Lindemann: Laying the cornerstone

As is generally conceded, the origins of crisis theory lie in Lindeman's classic study of grief reactions (1944). Lindemann reported on the evaluation and treatment of 101 persons, all of whom had recently experienced the death of a close relative. A number of these people were victims or close relatives of victims of Boston's Coconut Grove nightclub fire, which claimed almost five hundred lives in 1942. As though to lay the cornerstone for future theoretical and clinical understanding of human crises, Lindemann observed that acute grief was "a normal reaction to a distressing situation," and moreover that such reactions presented remarkably uniform and identifiable clinical pictures that appeared to form a distinct syndrome.

Normal grief reactions, as Lindemann posited, were generally acute, had an identifiable onset, and endured for only a relatively brief period. Furthermore, such reactions generally followed a predictable course that developed through a sequence of specific, identifiable stages. While serious psychopathology might appear as sequelae to these reactions, the reactions themselves, he was convinced, were ordinarily not pathological, but rather were more often transitory adjustment struggles aimed at mastery of a trying situation. Finally, and perhaps most importantly from a clinical point of view, Lindemann believed that the possibility of such psychopathological sequelae could be minimized by appropriate intervention directed toward helping the individual to identify, understand, and master the specific psychological tasks posed by the stressful situation.

Historically viewed, all these characteristics identified by Lindemann in 1944 remain significant aspects of the concept "crisis" as it is understood and used by more contemporary theorists and clinicians (Caplan, 1964; Rapoport, 1962; Darbonne, 1967; Kaplan, 1968; Eastham, Coates, and Allodi, 1970; Pasewark and Albers, 1972; Kardener, 1975). Lindemann referred to his innovative approach to the management of acute grief as "preventive intervention," its purpose being the prevention of more serious personality disturbance or psychopathology. Both theoretically and practically, there is little doubt that preventive intervention is the forerunner of contemporary crisis intervention.

Viewing optimistically the potential of preventive intervention for dealing clinically with other acute reactions to stress as well, Lindemann organized in 1948 the Wellesley (Massachusetts) Human Relations Service, a community mental health program designed as a clinical setting in which to explore and implement his preventive ideas. For five years a multidisciplinary team of mental health, public health, and social science professionals carried out a series of interrelated studies and service operations aimed at testing, modifying, and further articulating Lindemann's basic premises regarding the utility of preventive intervention (Klein and Lindemann, 1961).

Caplan: Erecting the framework

Lindemann's principal colleague at Wellesley, Gerald Caplan, has probably done more than any other to develop and articulate a theory of crisis with broad implications for clinical practice. Drawing upon the earlier formulations of Lindemann and others[1] as well as on his own experience and that of his colleagues both at Wellesley and (later) at the Harvard School of Public Health,[2] Caplan has provided the essential theoretical base upon which most current crisis intervention practice rests.

Caplan's crisis theory (1964) is grounded in the concept of emotional homeostasis. The individual, he says, is continually confronted with situations that threaten to upset the consistent pattern and balance of his emotional functioning. Ordinarily, however, such threats are short-lived in that the threatening situation is successfully mastered through habitual problem-solving activity. According to Caplan, although the individual is in a state of relative tension during the period prior to successful mastery, such tension is generally minimal, since this period is comparatively brief and the individual is aware, from past experience, that mastery is forthcoming.

Given mastery of the threatening situation with minimal self-awareness and strain through the use of habitual methods, the in-

1. Caplan refers in particular to the influence of the writings of Erik Erikson (1950, 1959) in regard to "developmental crises" (Caplan, 1964).
2. Among the researches reported by Caplan's group at the Harvard School of Public Health's Community Mental Health Program were studies of the reactions of parents to premature birth (Caplan, 1960; Kaplan and Mason, 1960; Kaplan, 1961), those of families to the diagnosis of tuberculosis in a family member (Parad and Caplan, 1960), and those of young couples adjusting to engagement, early marriage, and the birth of their first child (Rapoport, 1963).

dividual is said to have successfully coped with a "problem." Sometimes, however, the threatening situation is of such magnitude that it cannot be readily mastered by habitual methods of problem-solving. It is then, says Caplan, that the individual begins to experience "crisis."

In Caplan's purview, crisis refers to one's emotional reaction and not to the threatening situation itself. As such, crisis is naturally an individual matter. Caplan, however, identifies a number of situations that are commonly of sufficient threat as to precipitate this reaction: for example, loss of a loved one, addition of a family member, loss or change of job, threat to bodily or family integrity, change in social role, or entry into a new developmental life stage such as adulthood, marriage, or parenthood. Thus, in Caplan's view, the situational precipitant for crisis may be either "accidental" or "developmental." Whatever the situation, its potential as a precipitant of crisis is largely a function of how it is perceived by the individual. As Caplan suggests, the essential factor determining the occurrence of crisis is an imbalance between the perceived difficulty and significance of the threatening situation, and the resources available immediately for coping with the situation. When the individual perceives a situation as threatening the satisfaction of some fundamental need or needs, and circumstances are such that habitual problem-solving techniques are inadequate for mastery within reasonable time expectations, his reaction is one of crisis.

In describing the typical course of a crisis, Caplan identifies four distinct phases:

1. An initial phase in which the individual, confronted by a problem that poses a threat to certain of his needs, responds to feelings of increased tension by calling forth habitual problem-solving measures in an effort to solve the problem and restore emotional equilibrium.

2. If habitual measures fail and the problem and threat persist, tension further increases, producing feelings of upset

and ineffectuality. The individual's functioning becomes disorganized and he resorts to trial-and-error attempts at resolution and mastery.

3. With the continued failure of problem-solving efforts, a further rise in tension acts as a stimulus for the mobilization of emergency and novel problem-solving measures. The problem may be redefined so as to make it fit with past experience; certain aspects of it may be set aside as impossible but irrelevant; or the individual may resign himself to the problem, giving up certain of his goals as unattainable. Or, as a result of his mobilization of effort, the individual may solve the problem and restore emotional equilibrium.

4. If the problem continues and cannot be solved, surmounted, or avoided by any of the Phase 3 mechanisms, tension mounts beyond what Caplan calls the "breaking point," and major personality disorganization ensues.

In his discussion, Caplan cites the frequent observation that many patients suffering from mental disorder have previously undergone significant personality decompensation apparently during fairly short periods of crisis. Yet crisis, he maintains, is not in itself a pathological state, but rather a struggle for adjustment and adaptation in the face of problems that are for a time insoluble. Indeed, contends Caplan, crisis presents at once an opportunity for personality growth as well as a danger of increased vulnerability to psychopathology. Depending upon how the individual deals with the crisis, he may emerge from it more *or* less mentally healthy than he had been prior to its onset.

Caplan also identifies several other aspects of crisis that have particular relevance for therapeutic intervention:

1. Crises are generally self-limiting and will be resolved for better or worse within a period of from one to five weeks.

2. The outcome of crisis is generally not the result of antecedent factors such as the nature of the problem, the individual's personality, or his experience. While these fac-

tors may, as Caplan says, "load the dice" one way or the other, the actual outcome is dependent chiefly upon the actions of the subject and the intervention of others.

3. During crisis, the individual experiences an increased desire to be helped by others, and signals this to them in an effort to evoke a helping response.

4. During crisis, the individual is much more open and amenable to outside intervention than at times of stable functioning.

Beyond Caplan

Other clinician-theorists have expanded, articulated more fully, and in some instances modified Caplan's crisis model. Caplan's original theory, however, remains fundamental to these other formulations, and most of this additional work has been directed largely toward broadening or defining more clearly the clinical applicability of his model.

Klein and Lindemann (1961), for example, note that crisis does not occur in a social vacuum: an individual's crisis is often symptomatic of a crisis being experienced by one or more of his reference groups. Thus, maintain these authors, the basic unit of analysis in the understanding of crisis is not the individual subject but rather "one or more of the social orbits of which he is a member."

In particular, the role of the family in crisis has been singled out for attention. As Parad and Caplan (1960) point out, families may experience crisis much as individuals do. And just as Caplan describes the individual as more susceptible to outside intervention during crisis than at times of stable functioning, so families in crisis have been described by others (notably Waldfogel and Gardner, 1961; Rapoport, 1962; Kaffman, 1963).

Others, such as Rapoport (1962), note that crisis, while an emotional reaction to a present threat, may in part be rooted in, or at least directly affected by, the individual's past experience with threats to his basic needs. A present threat, Rapoport maintains, is often linked symbolically with former threats and is thus likely to "reactivate unresolved or partially resolved unconscious conflicts." Having failed to confront earlier threats successfully, apparently the individual may be at a particular disadvantage as he attempts to deal with current but similar threats. As Rapoport also points out, however, current crises may provide the individual with a "second chance" in that by dealing adaptively with a present threat he may be able to "correct earlier faulty problem-solving."

In addition, Rapoport spells out a pattern of responses necessary for the individual or family to resolve a crisis adaptively. Generally, she says, adaptive resolution (that which serves to strengthen the individual's or family's adaptive capacity) requires:

1. an accurate cognitive appraisal of the situation creating the crisis;

2. appropriate management of affect, including the identification and expression of feelings in ways that allow for tension reduction but do not interfere with mastery of the situation; and

3. a willingness to seek and accept the help of others in attempting to master the situation.

Crisis theory and more traditional frameworks

Crisis theory, as it has evolved through the works of Caplan and others, is remarkably consistent with a number of more traditional theoretical frameworks. Its emphasis on individual coping mechanisms, for example, has a direct parallel in ego psychology, which stresses the adaptive functions of the ego. Further, in viewing crisis as a state with potential for psychological growth, the theory has much in common with both humanistic and existential orientations as well. Then, too, its notion of crisis as a nearly automatic response to certain kinds of environmental stimuli renders crisis theory quite compatible with aspects of the behaviorist tradition. Finally, of course, in view of its concern for emotional homeostasis and tension reduction, as well as the symbolic links between present threats and those of the past, crisis theory is consistent with many aspects of the traditional psychoanalytic model of motivation and behavior.

Criticisms of crisis theory

While they appear to be few in number, crisis theory has not been without its critics. Taplin (1971), for example, taking issue with its basis in the concept of emotional homeostasis, notes that this concept has been widely criticized in psychology because it "limits psychological man to the status of reactor." Furthermore, he contends, this concept not only makes no distinction between adaptive and maladaptive emotional imbalance but it also fails to account adequately for important aspects of human behavior such as "growth, development, change and actualization" and has "nothing to say" about aspects of personality functioning such as feelings, ideas, and relationships.

Referring to emotional homeostasis as overly simplistic and "tenuous" as a basis for crisis theory, Taplin recommends rather that the state of crisis be conceived of in what he calls "cognitive" terms. The person in crisis, he maintains, is not simply reacting to an upsetting stimulus in a predictable way, but is rather suffering a temporary interruption of his cognitive processes, including the ability to "think, perceive, remember, evaluate situations, respond to people, make decisions," and so on. Successful resolution of a crisis, then, might be viewed as the restoration of these processes to normal functioning. This conceptualization, Taplin asserts, may well explain the observation that individuals sometimes resolve crises unassisted, apparently through their perseverance in calling upon old or designing new cognitive strategies for problem-solving.

Bartolucci and Drayer (1973) echo Taplin's criticisms and in addition score Caplan's contention that crises are universal phenomena and can be described independently of the individual's personality traits or other psychological capacities. They view as a major shortcoming in crisis theory what they regard as Caplan's "stimulus-response frame of reference." This frame of reference, they say, "discounts spontaneity" and the role it may play for individuals or groups facing disabling threats to their emotional well-being.

While these criticisms have been raised in good faith by serious practitioners, undoubtedly others would question their legitimacy, particularly in the light of Caplan's emphasis on novel problem-solving as a means to adaptive crisis resolution, and Rapoport's description of accurate cognitive appraisal as a precondition for such resolution. Indeed, despite these and other less telling criticisms, Caplan's conception of crisis remains in great part the basis for contemporary practice of crisis intervention. This is not to imply, of course, that crisis theory as developed by Caplan and his followers has inspired dogmatic acceptance and application among mental health practitioners. In fact, as will be seen in the chapters to follow, many clinicians have altered certain aspects of crisis theory to fit the unique demands of the clinical problems confronting them.

3

Clinical practice

As recounted in Chapter 2, Caplan and others have provided a firm theoretical basis for what has come to be known as crisis intervention. Yet for the most part the architects of crisis theory have not explicitly spelled out specific modes of intervention. As Pasewark and Albers (1972) note, "One assumes that the techniques to be used remain the prerogative of the intervenor."

The actual techniques and clinical principles of crisis intervention have developed over the past couple of decades out of the works of various clinicians. While these techniques and principles tend to be grounded in crisis theory, most of them appear to have developed rather independently, primarily through pragmatic efforts to meet the needs of particular client populations more effectively. As is widely acknowledged, for instance, much of the move toward short-term psychotherapies such as crisis intervention has been inspired by the mental health profession's need to meet an ever-growing demand for services with static or diminishing budgets and staffs. For many clients, however, especially those who do not respond well to traditional psychotherapy, crisis intervention has intrinsic value and is regarded as a treatment of choice. Questions relating to the efficacy of crisis intervention and its appro-

priateness as psychotherapy for various client populations are considered in detail in Chapters 6 and 7, respectively.

General principles

Although today there is an almost infinite variety of approaches to
crisis intervention practice, there are so many features common to
these approaches as to be regarded as general principles of such
practice.

1. *Crisis intervention is readily available and brief.* As was noted
in the preceding chapter, Caplan (1964) holds that crises are self-
limiting and endure for a period of no more than five weeks or so,
regardless of whether an adaptive resolution has been achieved.
He suggests further that people are more susceptible to external
intervention during crisis than at other times. In keeping with
these aspects of crisis theory, it is generally maintained that, to be
effective, crisis intervention must be readily available to the client
(Butcher and Maudal, 1976; Kardener, 1975; Hoffman and Remmel, 1975; Patterson and O'Sullivan, 1974; Schwartz, 1971; Wolkon, 1972; Kaplan, 1968; McGee, 1968; Parad and Parad, 1968;
Darbonne, 1967; Porter, 1966).

Availability of crisis intervention within twenty-four hours of the
client's initial application has often been regarded as optimal (Patterson and O'Sullivan, 1974). While few therapists have spoken
of an outside limit for the initiation of crisis intervention, Kardener (1975) suggests that a delay of two or more weeks in seeing
a client often means the loss of his "spontaneously generated re-
ceptivity" to treatment, thus sometimes precluding the efficacy of
a short-term therapy such as crisis intervention. Whatever the
delay involved, most clinicians would seem to agree with Parad
and Parad (1968) that if clients

> . . . in the midst of crisis have to wait for help the crisis may
> subside but perhaps with some crippling and sometimes tragic

results. A little bit of help at the right time may be more effective than a long period of help after the crisis has subsided.
(P. 420)

Interestingly, a minority of clinicians (e.g., Lang, 1974) seem to
feel that crisis intervention may benefit clients with chronic or
deeply entrenched problems as well as those with more acute difficulties—those who more closely fit Caplan's description of individuals in crisis. What little research there is on this important
question supports both the general and minority positions regarding the need to initiate treatment as soon as possible after onset
of the problem. This research (reviewed in some detail in Chapter
7) is about evenly divided between studies supporting the standard
requirement of immediate intervention (Shaw, Blumenfeld, and
Senf, 1968; Waldfogel and Gardner, 1961) and those failing to
find support for such a requirement (Ewing, 1975; Parad and Parad,
1968; Kaffman, 1963).

Since crisis intervention is generically a form of short-term psychotherapy, many clinicians have stressed the importance of setting specific time limits on the treatment. Frequently they have
pointed to the role that time limits play in enhancing and maintaining client motivation, particularly among lower socioeconomic
class clients who are less likely than others to expect or desire
lengthy psychotherapy.

While actual time limits vary greatly across agencies and clinicians, as Patterson and O'Sullivan (1974) note, the goals of most
programs of crisis intervention are ordinarily accomplished within
three to twelve sessions between client(s) and therapist. Crisis intervention clients, however, can and often do terminate therapy
abruptly and without notice. Setting an explicit contract with the
client may encourage him to continue with treatment for a predetermined number of sessions (Nelson and Mowry, 1976); yet,
as Butcher and Maudal (1976) warn, "all crisis psychotherapy sessions should be conducted as though they may be the last contact
with the patient."

Related to the issue of time limit is that of scheduling interviews in crisis intervention. In this regard, most crisis clinicans advocate flexibility and openness to the demands of the client's situation. As Hoffman and Remmel (1975) observe, crisis intervention interviews need not be limited to once a week, nor to fifty-minute hours.

2. *Crisis intervention deals not simply with individual clients but with families and social networks.* (Kardener, 1975; Bartolucci and Drayer, 1973; Pasewark and Albers, 1972). Crisis theorists, including Klein and Lindemann (1961) and Parad and Caplan (1960), have emphasized that crisis is rarely experienced by the individual alone but is ordinarily felt also by his family and the rest of his "social sphere" as well.

In keeping with this emphasis, as Schwartz (1971) notes, it has become virtually standard procedure to seek family and community involvement in the actual treatment process. The therapist actively encourages his clients to develop patterns of seeking and accepting help from interpersonal and institutional resources within the community (Rapoport, 1962; Ewalt, 1973). In addition, the therapist himself may enlist the aid of others in behalf of his clients (Butcher and Maudal, 1976). As a matter of course he may include significant others (especially family members) in the treatment sessions; he may request institutional services for the client from various community agencies; and he may serve as an advocate for the client in dealing directly with employers, schools, and/or other individuals and groups with whom the client is already involved.

3. *Crisis intervention addresses itself to no singular definition of crisis but rather to a wide range of human problems.* While Bloom (1963) has demonstrated that even highly skilled clinicians have great difficulty in agreeing upon the distinguishing features of the individual or family "in crisis," the current trend in most clini-

cal practice appears to be in the direction of greatly broadening the definition of those "in crisis" and hence suitable clients for crisis intervention. A number of clinicians have in fact taken the position that anyone requesting mental health services is *ipso facto* "in crisis" (Lang, 1974; Schwartz, 1971; Wolkon, 1972; Newman and San Martino, 1969).

Wolkon (1972) cites two arguments for defining such a request for help as a crisis. First of all, he notes, in seeking and accepting help from a practitioner whose help is not ordinarily sought, the client's situation is "a step away from normal" and as such represents a crisis. Secondly—and perhaps of greater significance from a practical point of view—Wolkon suggests that at the point of application for help, the client himself most often defines his situation as a crisis.

As Schwartz (1971) observes, while clinical definitions of crisis vary widely, such definitions are pragmatically of very little use to the clinician faced with an individual or family seeking help. Such clinician, he maintains, is presented with a crisis requiring intervention regardless of prior definitions.

Butcher and Maudal (1976), on the other hand, suggest that for practical purposes a distinction should be made between clients whose crises require psychotherapeutic intervention and clients who can be restored to emotional equilibrium through direct nonpsychotherapeutic intervention. Crisis intervention as psychotherapy, they maintain, should proceed only if in the therapist's judgment the client is likely both to require and to benefit from such intervention.

Others have taken similar positions. Kaplan (1968) and LaVietes (1974), for instance, argue that crisis intervention is not the treatment of choice for every client who presents himself for therapy. The therapist, they maintain, must exercise critical judgment in determining the appropriateness of a given client for crisis intervention. Unfortunately, to date, few have supplied very practical guidelines for making such determinations. The question of

which clients are appropriate for crisis intervention as psychotherapy is explored in greater detail in Chapter 7 of this volume.

4. *Crisis intervention is focused upon the client's present problems.* As is frequently emphasized, crisis intervention must focus
upon current problems, particularly those that precipitated the
client's request for help. According to both Kardener (1975) and
Chandler (1972), from the very start of the intervention the crisis
therapist directs his efforts most intensively toward determining
what changes in the client's life have led him to seek help at the
present time. That is, the therapist asks the client in many different ways, "Why now?"

In "uncovering the precipitant"—as Hoffman and Remmel
(1975) have named this aspect of crisis intervention—it is rarely
necessary or even useful to review the client's entire life history.
As Kardener notes, the crisis therapist is searching for "the straw
that broke the camel's back," and hence "a detailed exploration of
the prior 24 to 72 hours' sequence of events will usually suffice."
The traditional psychiatric history is generally too time-consuming
for short-term therapies such as crisis intervention, and often focused too narrowly upon the client's past to be of much help in
this regard. Whatever techniques are used to determine or uncover
the precipitant, crisis intervention rarely includes a full diagnostic
work-up.

Having "uncovered the precipitant," the crisis therapist takes
pains to maintain the client's attention to the problem(s) that
prompted him to seek help. Other problems derived from or
underlying the precipitant may be identified and related to the
initially identified problem(s). But the brief time available must
be clearly allocated to helping the client understand and deal with
the specific issues that led to treatment (Hoffman and Remmel,
1975). While either client or therapist may recognize other clinically meaningful issues of perhaps equal significance, the interven-

tion must maintain this narrow focus if the therapeutic effort is to be utilized most efficiently (Kardener, 1975).

5. *Crisis intervention seeks not only to resolve the presenting problem or "crisis" and to relieve symptoms, but also to help clients develop more adaptive mechanisms for coping with future problems and crises.* Although, as has been noted, crisis intervention is focused largely upon current problems, the crisis therapist nevertheless seeks to provide his clients with a basis for the adaptive resolution of other difficulties confronting or yet to confront them. As Parad (1965) stresses, the crisis therapist is interested in

> . . . utilizing the crisis situation to help those affected not only to solve present problems but also to become strengthened in mastering future vicissitudes by the use of more effective adaptive and coping mechanisms. (P. 2)

Thus, in a sense, the crisis therapist may be seen as helping the client to acquire coping skills useful not only at present but throughout the rest of his life. It is in this aspect that crisis intervention as psychotherapy comes closest to the psychiatric model of primary prevention advocated by Caplan (1964).

While crisis intervention and other forms of brief psychotherapy are frequently thought of primarily as offering only symptom relief, many crisis therapists expect and strive to bring about relatively lasting personality changes in their clients. Kaffman (1963), for example, while noting that the primary aim of family crisis intervention is "to bring the family to an emotional equilibrium as rapidly as possible with improvement or elimination of symptoms," believes that it is not unreasonable to expect such intervention to achieve "sustained changes in family dynamics and improvement of individual pathology." Likewise, Berlin (1970) sees crisis intervention as capable of bringing about "durable personality changes" that may "result in more integrative relations and more effective capacities for dealing with both internal conflicts and external realities."

6. *Crisis intervention is reality-oriented.* As Rapoport (1962) notes, an essential task for the crisis therapist is to enable his client to develop and maintain clear, correct cognitive perceptions of his situation. Thus, most crisis therapists take active measures to keep their therapeutic interactions with a client focused on the realities of his current situation and his role in creating and maintaining this situation.

Perhaps foremost in this regard, the crisis therapist strives to enable the client to confront directly the reality of his situation, discouraging the use of denial, avoidance, or projection (Schwartz, 1971). While continually offering emotional support, the crisis therapist may find it helpful, if not essential, to confront his client with the unrealistic or maladaptive nature of his goals, lifestyle, or belief system and to point out the possible negative consequences of current behavior patterns (Butcher and Maudal, 1976). And while communicating hope and optimism as to the client's ability to handle his problems, the crisis therapist takes pains to avoid giving the client false reassurance (Schwartz, 1971).

In addition, many crisis therapists find information-giving and limit-setting helpful in maintaining the realistic focus of the intervention. Offering the client realistic, factual information often serves to dispel "mythical beliefs" or cognitive misperceptions that have contributed to the difficulties for which he has sought treatment (Pasewark and Albers, 1972). The setting of firm limits within the therapeutic context is viewed as important in helping the client to realize the maladaptive and inappropriate nature of certain of his behaviors and ultimately to gain a measure of self-control over such behaviors (Butcher and Maudal, 1976).

Finally, the reality focus of crisis intervention applies not only to the client's cognitive perceptions but to his affective experiences and expressions as well. For example, catharsis has long been recognized by psychotherapists as a valuable experience for clients. Crisis therapists, however, generally do much more than simply offer a "safe" situation for the release of often highly-charged emotions: the client is also helped to keep his affects at a conscious level, where they can be clearly identified and managed through direct effort (Pasewark and Albers, 1972).

Here, just as in dealing with cognitive perceptions, confrontation may be an important clinical tool. Crisis therapists, for example, will often find it useful to confront the client with the maladaptive nature of certain affects, and to point out real or potential negative effects that the client's emotional reactions may have upon those around him. In addition, crisis therapists may give advice and make use of direct suggestion in helping their clients to understand better and manage more effectively—if not overcome— feelings detrimental to themselves or their interpersonal relations.

7. *Crisis intervention requires therapists to take non-traditional roles in dealing with their clients.* As Porter (1966), Sebolt (1973), and Patterson and O'Sullivan (1974) all assert, the crisis therapist (unlike the traditionally passive, psychoanalytically oriented therapist) must play an active, direct, involved role in the intervention. Indeed, as Butcher and Maudal (1976) note, "traditional attitudes of therapists such as 'objective' (aloof), 'disinterested' (noninvolved) and 'nondirective' (inefficient) are not appropriate in the crisis context."

The crisis therapist must show his own feelings, reactions, and involvement and not merely reflect on what the client says or does (Sebolt, 1973). Further, he must continually speculate (aloud) about his client's motives, intentions, vulnerabilities, resources, and unspoken needs and feelings, turning to him regularly for validation while encouraging him to disagree where appropriate (Berlin, 1970).

Crisis therapists, though influenced primarily in their practice by crisis theory, may bring any one or more of a number of clinical orientations to bear upon their clients' problems. Hoffman and Remmel (1975), for instance, suggest that such therapists have successfully applied techniques derived from sources as diverse as psychoanalytic theory, transactional analysis, communications and family-systems theory. Whatever his clinical orientation, however, the crisis therapist must be pragmatic and willing to utilize any resource leading to a healthier adjustment for his clients (Kaffman, 1963).

In thus taking a pragmatic stance, the crisis therapist must feel comfortable playing such non-traditional roles as educator, counselor, advisor (Weinberger, 1971; Kaffman, 1963), partner and model (Sebolt, 1973). And as Weinberger (1971) stresses, the crisis therapist must be able to take the view—"almost antithetical" to traditional insight therapy—that changes initiated in behavior can lead to increased understanding, self-awareness, and self-esteem.

8. *Crisis intervention may serve to prepare the client for further treatment.* While for most clients a brief regimen of crisis intervention proves adequate, a fairly substantial proportion appear to need, if not desire, further treatment. Thus, for many of them crisis intervention though useful in its own right may serve as a stepping-stone to long-term psychotherapy or to the utilization of other therapeutic services.

As Kaffman (1963) and Hoffman and Remmel (1975) observe, for some clients the request for further treatment reflects merely a resistance to, or an attempt to manage their affective responses to, termination of the brief intervention. Still, as these and other clinicians also recognize, for some clients the request for continued treatment is natural and appropriate, may be viewed as a positive therapeutic sign, and should be encouraged by the therapist.

Kardener (1975) views the "sense of success and accomplishment" often engendered by a positive experience with crisis intervention as encouraging the client to undertake further, more extensive, therapy, either immediately upon termination of the crisis contacts or at some later date. Indeed, as Ewalt (1973) notes, clients who have previously undergone crisis intervention often seem to respond more favorably to long-term psychotherapy than clients who have had no such prior experience.

4

Current uses of crisis intervention as psychotherapy

As a form of short-term psychotherapy, crisis intervention is widely used in a variety of clinical settings—most commonly in child and family treatment, as a form of marital therapy, and as a measure designed to avoid or shorten the psychiatric hospitalization of adults. Other less common though interesting uses of crisis intervention as psychotherapy include treatment of rape victims, juvenile offenders, homosexuals, drug addicts, and emergency-room patients, as well as a large and growing number of other special client populations.

Child and family crisis intervention

In what is probably the widest survey of utilization ever conducted in the field of crisis intervention, Parad and Parad (1968) queried 457 child and family treatment agencies as to their use of this modality. Of the 314 clinics belonging to the Family Service Association of America, 54, or 17.2 percent, reported offering "crisis-oriented planned short-term treatment." The remaining 143 clinics, all of which belonged to the American Association of Psychiatric Services for Children, included 44, or 30.8 percent, offering such treatment.

The number and percentage of other such clinics currently offering crisis intervention treatment is not known. In the years since the Parad survey, however, a number of new child-family crisis intervention programs have been described in the literature of psychology, psychiatry, and social work (e.g., Shaw, Blumenfeld, and Senf, 1968; Newman and San Martino, 1969; Berlin, 1970; Weinberger, 1971; and Kissel, 1974). Ewalt (1973) has also described a child-family crisis intervention psychotherapy program developed and operated in a large suburban child guidance clinic and serving over a third of the agency's total clientele (described in some detail in Chapter 5).

As LaVietes (1974) and others have noted, a frequent motive for the adoption of crisis intervention techniques in child guidance work has been the desire to maximize the utility of limited clinical resources. Another motive seems to be the continuing concern of child psychiatric facilities not only to provide care for groups that have not traditionally received it (notably, the poor and Black) but also to shorten the waiting period for those groups traditionally requesting and receiving care. As Ewing (1975) has observed, the cost of traditional child guidance treatment may be as much as ten times greater than that of child-family crisis intervention, despite his finding that the two treatments may achieve essentially the same results. Furthermore, as Ewalt (1973) notes, the "dropout" rate in family crisis intervention seems to be less than half that commonly found in traditional child guidance work.

Marital crisis intervention

While family crisis intervention in child guidance and family service agencies often involves some focus on the parents' marital situation, many agencies also use crisis intervention as a specific short-term approach to marriage counseling itself. In some agencies, marital crisis intervention is a planned alternative to more traditional modes of marriage counseling. Fallon (1973), for example, has described the regular use of crisis intervention as psychotherapy for marital partners in a family service agency.

In other agencies, crisis intervention seems to have become a form of marital therapy as a result of the frequent inclusion of a client's spouse in the treatment process. Ancell (1972), describing the experience of a general crisis intervention agency with a situation of this kind, reports that while over 50 percent of marital partners accompanied their spouses to treatment interviews, most did not regard themselves as objects of treatment and reported coming only to cooperate in or provide information for the treatment of their mate. In still other agencies, crisis intervention may concentrate upon the individual, the family, or the marital dyad, depending upon the therapist's assessment of the nature of the presenting problem (Hoffman and Remmel, 1975).

Whatever an agency's policy regarding its use as such, crisis intervention seems to be chosen frequently as an alternative to traditional marriage counseling. Aside from the obvious saving of time and agency resources, this particular use of crisis intervention appears motivated, at least in part, by the observation that many clients, particularly husbands, seem to need a short, time-limited contract in order to maintain their commitment to treatment. As Lang (1974) notes in describing one agency's experience, husbands who drop out of traditional long-term marital treatment, tend to remain committed throughout time-limited crisis intervention contacts, "possibly because their own 'male' need for mastery and control is not threatened." This conclusion is supported by the empirical findings of Reid and Shyne (1969), who compared brief and extended casework with couples.

Crisis intervention as an alternative to hospitalization

Psychiatric hospitalization is by far the least economical form of mental health treatment. In some cases the need for hospitalization is apparent and there may be no suitable alternative. But there is a growing body of evidence suggesting that, for many cases, brief crisis intervention (costing a fraction of the expense involved in hospitalization) may help prevent or at least reduce the duration of the hospitalization. In recent years a number of programs offering crisis intervention as an alternative to hospitalization have been described.

Interest in the use of crisis intervention techniques in this regard was sparked by the pioneering work of Langsley and Kaplan (1968). Langsley and Kaplan report having randomly assigned to outpatient family crisis intervention half of a group of 300 patients applying for psychiatric hospitalization. While all patients in the other half of the group were hospitalized, the need for hospitalization was avoided in all 150 crisis intervention cases. Not surprisingly, treatment costs for the hospitalized group were six times greater than those for the group treated with crisis intervention.

Crisis intervention has also more recently been utilized both during and after hospitalization in an effort to prevent or at least reduce subsequent hospital stays. Decker and Stubblebine (1972), for instance, followed up two groups of young adults for two years following their initial psychiatric hospitalizations. One group ($N = 315$) had received traditional psychiatric treatment only. For the other group ($N = 225$), hospitalization began with an effort to deal with presenting problems by means of crisis intervention. The follow-up indicated, among other things, that those patients whose hospitalization had included crisis intervention spent significantly fewer days in the hospital and were significantly less likely to have been rehospitalized.

In a related study, Rubinstein (1972) utilized crisis intervention with formerly hospitalized psychiatric patients in an effort to prevent their rehospitalization. During one six-month period, Rubinstein and his colleagues treated twenty-seven such patients with crisis intervention, avoiding re-admission for twenty-four of them. Prevention of rehospitalization in these cases is viewed by

Rubinstein as a direct result of the crisis intervention provided them.

As is discussed in Chapter 6, studies such as these are clearly not without methodological difficulties that make any interpretation of their findings hazardous. Certainly the works of these investigators cannot be seen as establishing that crisis intervention is a superior treatment alternative to psychiatric hospitalization. Their real value lies in their suggestion that routine, costly psychiatric hospitalization can be avoided or at least minimized through the careful use of relatively inexpensive treatment alternatives such as crisis intervention. Given the current economics of mental health service delivery, such a suggestion should be good news for most mental health professionals, administrators, politicians and taxpayers.

Crisis intervention with special client populations

In recent years, there has been a growing emphasis on the use of crisis intervention as the treatment of choice for a number of client populations—those with special problems heretofore given little therapeutic attention by the mental health professions. To a large extent the rationale for such use of crisis intervention has been the belief that these clients are, by the very nature of their problems, in crisis at the time they seek help and are thus most likely to benefit from psychotherapy with a short-term crisis orientation. Crisis intervention as psychotherapy for rape victims, juvenile offenders, homosexuals, drug addicts, and emergency room patients is emphasized here because of the growing social and statistical significance of these groups in contemporary society.

Rape victims Rape appears to be the fastest rising crime of violence in America today. FBI Uniform Crime Reports indicate that rape increased 68 percent (from 31,000 to 51,000 reported cases) between 1968 and 1973. Although rape has long been recognized among laymen as an emotionally traumatic crisis, explicit recognition of this common-sense observation by mental health professionals has come about only relatively recently and apparently with a good deal of reluctance.

Professional recognition of the psychological crisis of rape has in recent years led to the establishment of a number of crisis intervention programs specifically designed to aid victims of rape. These programs, in addition to insuring appropriate medical services, also often provide brief psychotherapy for rape victims, based upon the general principles of crisis theory.

One such program is described by McCombie, Bassuk, Savitz, and Pell (1976) as a "rape crisis intervention program" initiated as a regular service in a large metropolitan general hospital and staffed by specially trained psychologists, psychiatrists, nurses, and social workers. As part of this program, crisis therapists, who are on call twenty-four hours a day, provide immediate counseling for rape victims, accompany them throughout all emergency-room medical procedures, and schedule follow-up sessions with them within forty-eight hours of the initial contact.

The role of the crisis therapist in this program is to provide emotional support and information for the victim as well as for relatives and friends and to encourage medical personnel to respond sensitively to her psychological needs. As to the duration, frequency, content, and goals of such intervention, McCombie et al. indicate that

> Subsequent contacts are made at regular intervals for at least one year. The frequency and content of the intervention is based upon the needs of the victim, as determined by clinical assessment and timing of anticipated periods of exacerbation of symptoms, such as court appearances. The counseling goal is to increase the individual's adaptive capacity by delineating and working through the crisis-related issues. (P. 419)

Similar programs of crisis intervention as psychotherapy for the victims of rape have been described by Crum (1974), Burgess and Holmstrom (1974), and Fox and Scherl (1972).

Juvenile offenders. Mental health professionals have a long history of interest and involvement, but a rather poor track record in the field of juvenile delinquency. A major problem in the mental health treatment of juvenile offenders has been that treatment has often been available to such youngsters and their families only after they have become deeply involved with the juvenile justice system. A recent and encouraging trend away from this tradition, however, has included the provision of access to mental health services for such youths and their families upon their initial involvement with law enforcement agencies. The notion behind this trend, of course, is that early intervention may have great preventive impact.

One of the more recent aspects of this move toward prevention has been the development of crisis-oriented treatment approaches for youngsters and families who have just become involved with the law for the first time. Stratton (1975) has described one such approach developed on a pilot basis in a major metropolitan area.

This approach essentially involved initiating family crisis intervention with a juvenile and his parents within a few hours of the youth's initial arrest or detainment. In all, thirty families were treated by two professional counselors, one of whom was a psychologist. Emphasis in the treatment sessions (the average number of which was 2.5) was limited to the immediate problem: the youth's arrest and its effects upon him and his family. The intervention had as its goal the resolution of immediate problems created by the arrest, and the restoration of the family to its level of functioning prior to the arrest.

Utilizing a problem-solving orientation that is common to crisis intervention practice, the counselors worked with each family in an effort to promote:

1. Intellectual understanding of the problem by the minor and the family.
2. Expression of feelings related to the arrest and its impact on family members.
3. Exploration of the coping mechanisms attempted before arrest by the minor and his family.
4. Examination of why the coping mechanisms used before arrest were not working.
5. Consideration of various alternatives for the minor and family along with exploration of new methods of coping. (P. 10)

The results of Stratton's pilot project (which are reviewed critically and in more detail in Chapter 6) are encouraging. Those offenders who received family crisis intervention, as compared with thirty others processed more traditionally by the juvenile justice system, were found upon a six-month follow-up to have committed fewer offenses, to have been arrested and detained less frequently, and to have made less use of other probation department services. Moreover, the cost of this program per case was less than half the cost of traditional means for handling such cases.

Homosexuals The treatment or "mistreatment" of homosexuals by mental health professionals has long been an area of great controversy. For many years, homosexuality was regarded as a form of mental illness. Although officially this is no longer so, many professionals still seem to regard homosexuals and their problems in stereotyped, if not biased, ways.

Often this clinical stereotype or bias has been expressed in the assumption that homosexuals who seek psychiatric treatment are unhappy with their sexual orientations and that long-term psychotherapy is invariably indicated. While this assumption is sometimes valid, there appears to be a growing awareness among mental health professionals that many homosexuals seek help for the same reasons as others and that they, too, can benefit from short-term therapy such as crisis intervention. Atkins, Fischer, Prater, Winget, and Zaleski (1976), for instance, have recently reported on the promising results they obtained using crisis intervention with sixteen homosexual clients.

Though they deliberately excluded clients seeking a change in their sexual orientation, Atkins et al. report that these sixteen clients were all dealing with the same kinds of crises that afflict all people. As is often the case with clients seeking therapy, loss or threatened loss was the most common precipitant of their requests for help. Some of these clients were confronting loss of a love relationship. Others were faced with potential loss of employment, family support, friends, or self-esteem surrounding their decisions to "come out" or make public their homosexuality.

Like most crisis therapists, the therapists treating these clients tried to help them deal with their problems in realistic and adaptive ways. At times this meant attempting to strengthen supportive homosexual relationships, encouraging acceptance on the part of the client's family, taking steps to reduce feelings of guilt over homosexuality, and helping the client to make contact with community groups supportive of the "gay" cause.

In all, Atkins and her colleagues acknowledge that providing crisis intervention for homosexual clients is not an easy task, but agree that such therapy can be just as beneficial to homosexuals as it is to heterosexuals.

Drug abusers   It has been argued in a recent volume on crisis intervention that mental health professionals frequently suffer from a "cultural bias" that precludes their effective treatment of cases presenting problems associated with drug abuse (Jaffe, 1973). Regardless of the validity of this charge, many professionals themselves evidently view the traditional tools of psychotherapy as inadequate and / or inappropriate for intervention in such cases. A number of mental health professionals, in fact, have turned to crisis intervention as possibly a more adequate and appropriate treatment modality for clients with drug-related problems.

Wellisch and Gay (1972), for example, have described a crisis intervention psychotherapy program for heroin addicts developed to fill a void in psychiatric services to such clients created by hospitals' unwillingness to admit addicts in need of psychiatric care. According to these authors, among the major difficulties confronting the crisis therapist treating addicts are these clients' unresponsiveness and particularly low self-esteem. They posit that in addition to overcoming these difficulties, the crisis therapist who would successfully treat addicts must first view them as treatable and recognize that their addiction may be both a cause and a result of social problems.

Others such as Mackenzie and Bruce (1972), Jaffe (1973), and Clark and Rootman (1974) have described a different, more common form of crisis intervention service for users and abusers of a wide variety of drugs. While these forms are loosely referred to as "crisis intervention," they do not appear to utilize crisis concepts in any explicitly psychotherapeutic way. Rather, like many "drug crisis centers" and "hotlines," they provide a mixed variety of services including information and referral, self-help groups, volunteer counseling, and emergency management of "bad trips."

Emergency-room patients In recent years, general hospital emergency rooms have become the primary source of health care and social services for many Americans. Today it is clear that as many as half of all emergency-room patients do not present what are considered to be "true emergencies." And even while the vast majority of these patients do present fairly specific somatic complaints, it is also clear that a substantial number are really seeking or in need of help for emotional or psychosocial problems (Nigro, 1970). Furthermore, a number of patients turn to hospital emergency rooms with the clear expectation of receiving psychiatric help (Kardener, 1975).

In an effort to cope with the growing use of emergency rooms as primary care facilities by patients with a wide range of emotional and psychosocial difficulties, many hospitals have begun instituting crisis intervention programs as a regular part of their emergency-room functions. Two such programs have been described by Hankoff, Mischorr, Tomlinson, and Joyce (1974) and Bartolucci and Drayer (1973).

While describing the emergency rooms of general hospitals as ideal sites for crisis intervention programs, these authors hasten to warn of factors that clearly hinder the development of such programs in these traditionally medical settings:

1. Traditional concepts of injury and illness, which often dominate the thinking of emergency-room medical personnel, are geared toward immediate response to clearly "definable medical emergencies" and thus may limit the responsiveness of such personnel to the often ill-defined, poorly articulated, and non-emergent problems presented by clients in crisis.

2. Limitations of space and time may preclude extended initial interventions as well as direct follow-up of cases by emergency room personnel.

3. Medically trained workers often regard psychological problems as outside their professional domain and tend to refer such problems to mental health facilities.

Despite these real obstacles, the above authors remain confident that emergency-room personnel can make the "formidable leap from theory to practice" and develop viable crisis intervention programs for their patients. Their experience, however, seems to suggest that several key features are essential to the successful development of these programs:

1. "Mature" professional staffs with both medical and psychological training and experience (Hankoff et al. suggest that emergency room staff nurses, given appropriate psychiatric supervision and consultation, may function as ca-

pable crisis therapists, while Bartolucci and Drayer stress the need for a "medico-psycho-social" team composed of psychiatrist, psychiatric nurse, and social worker);

2. Flexible staffing arrangements which allow for adequate case follow-through (including additional interviews, phone calls, and referrals) after the initial emergency room contact; and

3. A treatment orientation which, in keeping with the principles of crisis theory, gives appropriate consideration to the social, economic and cultural impact of the family, community and the emergency-room setting itself, upon the client's functioning.

Although no clear empirical evidence of the efficacy of emergency-room crisis intervention is yet available, Hankoff and his colleagues report that many of their patients appear to have benefited from such intervention. They note further that only five of their forty patients required referral for additional psychiatric treatment. The finding that four of these five were successfully placed in further treatment is in itself evidence of the value of crisis intervention. As these authors note, "it is a well-known fact that ordinarily, referrals to clinics (particularly to the psychiatric clinic from the emergency room) have a low degree of success."

Others. In addition to its psychotherapeutic uses with rape victims, juvenile offenders, homosexuals, drug abusers, and emergency-room patients, crisis intervention as short-term psychotherapy has also been utilized with a variety of other special client populations, among them cardiac outpatients (Golden, Golden, and Dibiase, 1972), drinking drivers (Sackman, 1972), adolescents (Christ, 1972; Patrick and Wander, 1974), the elderly (Sadler, 1973), families of the critically ill (Werhan, 1973), Mexican-Americans (Serrano and Gibson, 1973), disaster victims (Goldsmith and Zeitlin, 1973), college students (Weiss and Kapp, 1974), child-abusing parents (Ten Broeck, 1974), and unwed pregnant teen-agers (Stone, 1975).

5

Three crisis intervention programs

As observed at the start of the preceding chapter, the most common psychotherapeutic uses of crisis intervention appear to be in child and family treatment, as a form of marital therapy, and as a measure designed to avoid or shorten the psychiatric hospitalization of adults. The crisis intervention programs developed and utilized by three large clinical facilities provide excellent examples of the use of this therapeutic modality in each of these ways.

In child-family treatment: The "Crisis Clinic"

A frequently described program is that of the Framingham (Massachusetts) Youth Guidance Center (FYGC), a family-oriented child guidance clinic (Ewalt and Cohen, 1971; Ewalt, 1973; Ewing, 1975; Ewing, 1976). This family crisis-intervention service, known as the "Crisis Clinic," was initiated in 1971 in an effort to "deal with the dissatisfaction of clients and community professionals who had encountered delays in service (Ewalt, 1973)." The Crisis Clinic's services are not limited to families "in crisis," but are provided to a wide variety of clients, roughly one-third of all FYGC applicants, or between 200 and 250 families annually.

The therapeutic approach of the Crisis Clinic utilizes a model of crisis intervention suggested by Rapoport (1962) based upon the writings and teachings of Lindemann and Caplan (see Chapter 2). Rapoport's model, which describes the three tasks of the crisis therapist, has been summarized by Ewalt (1973), one of the founders of the Crisis Clinic. According to Ewalt,

1. The worker attempts to collaborate with the family to attain a cognitive grasp of the family's salient problems;

2. He attempts to foster an awareness in each family member of his own and others' affective responses causing and resulting from the problem;

3. He attempts to mobilize the resources of the individual family members, of the family as a whole, and of the community, including further services of the clinic or other resources. (P. 407)

Since the Crisis Clinic is part of FYGC's ongoing program of clinical services, its cases are drawn from the general applicant pool. Whether a family is assigned to the "Crisis Clinic" for short-term family crisis intervention, or to the center's more traditional child guidance program for evaluation and possible long-term treatment, depends upon such factors as the length of current waiting lists for evaluation and treatment, current availability of staff and trainee therapists, and the judgment of the worker screening applications.

The Crisis Clinic adheres to an immediately accessible, time-limited, one-worker approach to family crisis intervention. The applicant (usually the mother) being assigned to the Clinic is told during the screening call that an appointment is available, most often within a few days, and that a clinic worker will meet with the family "for up to four hours of interview time to help you understand the problem and figure out what to do about it" (Ewalt, 1973, p. 408).

For the initial interview it is expected that the identified child client, both parents, and occasionally other significant family members and/or friends will be present. At this time the family meets with the therapist with whom they will be working, and the four-hour period begins. This four-hour limit was chosen because it coincides with the number of hours ordinarily spent on intake and diagnostic interviews in traditional child guidance practice at FYGC. Rarely do Crisis Clinic cases require more than four hours, and often much less time is utilized.

How the four hours are to be spent (including the length, number, and intervals between interviews, as well as the family members to be included in each interview) is planned purposefully by the therapist in consultation with one of the two senior workers who supervise the Crisis Clinic's operation. Time used aside from in-person interviews is not counted in the four-hour limit, nor is it restricted. Psychological testing is used in about a third of the cases, and case recording and conference time averages about 6.5 hours per case. Conferences may involve collaboration with other clinic personnel and community professionals, but generally are not formal progress or dispositional conferences.

Once the four-hour intervention is concluded, further treatment for the family is not ruled out. Some families are offered further services at FYGC, some are referred to other community sources (e.g., social service agencies, school guidance counselors), and some receive no further services or referral. In all cases, however, termination involves an assessment of the family's need, suitability, and willingness for additional help.

Not surprisingly, the family crisis intervention (FCI) approach of the Crisis Clinic contrasts strikingly with the center's traditional child guidance (TCG) approach. To begin with, FCI is provided almost immediately upon request for service, but for TCG cases there is often a wait of at least a week between application and initial interview. Secondly, while FCI is time-limited from the start, TCG clients generally receive little concrete indication of the length of time that treatment may require. Third, while FCI involves one clinic worker per case, TCG ordinarily involves an intake worker, a diagnostic worker, and as many treatment workers as may be required by the specific therapeutic plan developed for the clients. Fourth, while TCG cases are formally conferenced at the end of the intake-diagnostic phase, at intervals throughout treatment, and again prior to termination, FCI cases are rarely conferenced, their dispositions being at the discretion of the worker in consultation with one of the Crisis Clinic supervisors.

Finally, and perhaps most importantly, FCI and TCG differ radically in their approach to the problems presented by the child and parents. FCI is focused on the problem that brought the family to the clinic. The guiding notion, drawn from crisis theory, is that the family's troubles represent not so much psychopathology or personality disturbance as a temporary inability to cope adaptively with a disruptive problem or "crisis." TCG, on the other hand, is based upon more traditional psychoanalytic principles that posit the family's difficulties as symptomatic of underlying, often deeply entrenched, unconscious conflicts within and among family members.

There can be little doubt that, at least as practiced at FYGC, family crisis intervention has definite economic advantages over traditional child guidance modalities. In one study conducted at FYGC, Ewing (1975) found that while TCG treatment averaged 36.5 interview hours per family, FCI averaged only 3.5 interview hours. Translating time into dollars and cents, the cost of TCG to client and clinic was more than ten times greater than that of FCI. Findings such as these help a great deal to explain Ewalt's earlier finding (1973) that, while the dropout rate in FYGC's traditional child guidance program is roughly 50 percent (i.e., half the client families cease clinic contacts during intake / evaluation or before treatment can begin), the same rate for Crisis Clinic cases is only 11 percent.

Finally, there is some evidence—albeit far from conclusive—to suggest that, despite its brevity and relatively low cost, family crisis intervention may be no less effective for FYGC clients than the more time-consuming and expensive traditional child guidance approach. Ewing's study (reviewed in further detail in Chapter 6) also found no significant differences in outcome between one group of cases treated with FCI and another group that had received TCG.

In a family service agency: "Crisis Psychotherapy"

The Family Service of Milwaukee (FSM) is the site of another program utilizing crisis intervention as psychotherapy. This program, labeled "Crisis Psychotherapy" and offered to a variety of clients including married couples, is described in full detail by Hoffman and Remmel (1975).

The Crisis Psychotherapy program at FSM developed as a result of two separate but related stimuli. First, the staff of the agency was impressed with Caplan's (1964) crisis theory and its implications for time-limited psychotherapy. Second, and of more practical significance, they recognized that two-thirds of their clients were coming to the agency no more than five times and that this was not a sign of motivational lack but rather of a desire for quick, economical help.

Crisis Psychotherapy at FSM is available to all clients, including families, couples, and individuals, since, as Hoffman and Remmel observe, "it is assumed that all clients calling the agency for an appointment are in a state of crisis." Upon calling, each client or group of clients is randomly assigned to a staff member, who takes the initial application and becomes the ongoing therapist. Usually the client is offered a first appointment within a few days of his call. The number, length, and duration of treatment interviews varies and there are no arbitrary limits. About one-third of these clients require and desire additional long-term treatment. In such cases,

Crisis Psychotherapy is viewed as the beginning phase of a long-term treatment contract.

As conceptualized at FSM, Crisis Psychotherapy proceeds in three stages. The initial phase is ordinarily carried out during the first interview, which encompasses the intake process as well as the start of treatment and frequently requires at least two hours. The chief tasks at this phase are to identify the presenting problem and precipitating event and, most importantly, the "uncovering of the precipitant." The "precipitant," according to Hoffman and Remmel,

> is not synonymous with the terms *precipitating event* (which is the final blow in the chain of events that converts an emotionally hazardous situation into a state of crisis) or *emotional hazard* or *hazardous event* (which refers to the initial event, blow, or change that sets off a series of reactions leading to a crisis). The precipitant is the thought or feeling aroused by the precipitating event. Although related to the precipitating event, it is distinct from it and more highly repressed. It is the pain connected with the earlier unresolved conflict, and it is precisely this experience that impels the client to pick up the telephone to call for help. (P. 260)

Once the "precipitant" has been identified, a contract for a specific number of interviews is generally made with the client. The "precipitant" provides the focus for subsequent interviews, and "client and therapist move into the middle phase of crisis psychotherapy" (p. 264).

This middle phase provides an "empathic milieu" in which the client may give vent to pent-up feelings, and an "intellectual framework" that will enable the client to develop a "cognitive grasp" of his situation. Therapists at FSM are free to utilize any of a number of theoretical approaches in providing this "milieu" and "framework." Transactional analysis, psychoanalytic concepts and techniques, and communications theory approaches are among

those commonly employed. Whatever approach is used, the therapist is careful to maintain the therapeutic focus on the crisis or
conflict identified in the initial interview. Other problems or conflicts may be significant, but when raised by the client at this
phase, they are thought best interpreted as "resistance to fully
facing the current conflict or as a defense against termination of
therapy" (p. 265).

The third and final phase involves termination. While termination in Crisis Psychotherapy is never unexpected—given the usual
nature of the short-term treatment contract—it often remains a
difficult aspect of treatment for both client and therapist. None-
theless, as Hoffman and Remmel assert (p. 266), "just as it is the
therapist's job to insist on facing the precipitant, it is also his job,
at termination, to face his and his clients' pain at separating."

"Successful" termination in Crisis Psychotherapy involves not
only an honest facing and understanding of this pain but also a
realistic appraisal of the client's need for, motivation toward, and
ability to benefit from further treatment beyond the short-term
"crisis" contract. Hoffman and Remmel stress that while Crisis
Psychotherapy in no way hinders subsequent long-term treatment,
such additional therapy is indicated "only if the client both needs
and wants it." Their experience at FSM indicates that the vast
majority of Crisis Psychotherapy clients do not desire further
treatment.

Like the Crisis Clinic described in the preceding section, FSM's
Crisis Psychotherapy program has sharply decreased the number
of early client dropouts. Prior to the initiation of this program,
only 60–67 percent of FSM clients returned to the agency for a
second interview. A full 80 percent of Crisis Psychotherapy clients
return for additional interviews. And even among the 20 percent
who do not return, there is reason to believe that they have already been helped by a single session of Crisis Psychotherapy.

At the same time the program has greatly increased FSM's fee
income. Prior to instituting this program, it was assumed that

since all clients were potential candidates for long-term treatment, minimal fees should be charged to enable them to afford such treatment. Under the Crisis Psychotherapy program it is assumed that all applicants for service are potential short-term clients and, thus, should be willing and able to afford higher fees. This policy change has resulted in a doubling of FSM's fee income over a period of three years.

In addition to economic considerations, there is also evidence that the Crisis Psychotherapy program may be even more effective than traditional psychotherapeutic approaches employed earlier at FSM. Hoffman and Remmel, for example, report that

> a one-year followup of cases revealed a statistically significant reported improvement in the marital-sexual relationships and in improved feelings about the self in cases treated with crisis psychotherapy as opposed to the control cases treated with traditional methods. (P. 260)

As an alternative to hospitalization: The "Grady Psychiatric System"

The "Grady Psychiatric System" at Atlanta's Grady Hospital has been the site of a family crisis-intervention program aimed at preventing or at least reducing the duration of psychiatric hospitalization. This program, which has been described by Chandler (1972), handles the bulk of twelve thousand or more new applicants to the "System" annually. While the program is essentially an outpatient clinic operation, special services including inpatient treatment (averaging five days) are available when needed.

Family crisis-intervention clients in the Grady System are seen as a family, generally by two co-therapists, each from a different professional discipline and, wherever possible, one male and one female. The rationale for this arrangement is that, in Chandler's words, it exposes clients to "a broader spectrum of possible relationships and a wider opportunity for common interest" than might be had with a single therapist or two therapists of the same sex and professional orientation. Typically, client families are seen for a "flexible maximum" of six to eight visits, one of which is usually held in the family home. On occasion "multiple therapy configurations" are used, and a family is split in various ways into sessions with one or both therapists.

Diagnosis is deemed irrelevant in the decision to provide a given client with outpatient crisis intervention as opposed to other possible dispositions. The family crisis intervention program is open to all "System" clients except cases in which: 1. neither therapist is able to establish a meaningful relation with the identified client or his family; 2. there are no other sources of emotional support outside the "System"; or 3. the identified client or another family member is "*impulsively* homicidal or suicidal."

As with other programs of crisis intervention, the Grady System begins with an effort to determine the factors that have precipitated the application for help: treatment begins for each family when a therapist asks, "Why now?" Initially, information regarding precipitating factors is gathered from as many sources as possible: immediate and extended family, referral source, and other agencies or individuals interested in the client or his family. This emphasis on the current crisis, the "here and now," begins with the first contact and is maintained throughout the intervention.

In addition to this focus, common to most crisis intervention methods, Grady therapists also maintain a focus on the family as the unit of treatment during all aspects of the intervention. From the very first contact, they work to shift the focus from the identified client to the entire family. They redefine the "client's problem" as a family crisis and endeavor to explore family dynamics, roles, rules, relationships, and responsibilities. This family orientation is frequently reinforced and concretized through the prescription of behavioral tasks and even medication for family members as well as for the identified client.

The early stages of the intervention are marked not only by efforts to make the family aware of the nature of the crisis and their collective role in preventing or avoiding its successful resolution, but also by the provision of a heavily supportive and highly directive therapeutic milieu. Therapists take an "active problem-solving approach" and are "aggressive" in their efforts to define the crisis, promote discussion and compromise, and assign specific tasks to family members.

By contrast, in the middle stage of intervention just prior to termination, therapists become increasingly less supportive and directive, often dropping the "therapist role" as the end of treatment approaches. Termination, considered the crucial stage in the Grady program, involves an effort to arrive at "a meaningful resolution" of dependency needs and conflicts, and to allow the family to leave treatment secure in its own "capacity for handling future stresses and the inevitable crises of life." Efforts are made to deal with the feelings of both clients and therapists surrounding termination and the loss it involves. As Chandler observes, an "ideal termination" to family crisis intervention at Grady may be said to have occurred when all parties involved can say, "I feel sad, mad and glad and that's not bad."

While, as Chandler reports, most cases are not terminated in "ideal" fashion, there is some evidence that the program has had positive impact. According to Chandler, the institution of the family crisis intervention program at Grady was followed by a reduction in the percentage of clients referred to the state hospital for treatment from approximately 25 percent to less than 4 percent of those evaluated at Grady.

6

Evaluating crisis intervention

As the preceding chapters indicate, crisis intervention has become a widely used psychotherapeutic modality. As such, it has also become the object of growing scrutiny among researchers seeking to evaluate the efficacy of various programs of mental health treatment. The object of this chapter is to provide a brief critical review of current evidence regarding the efficacy of crisis intervention as psychotherapy.

Essentially this evidence has been derived from four sources: 1. anecdotal case and program reports; 2. uncontrolled outcome studies; 3. a single controlled outcome study; and 4. studies comparing crisis intervention outcomes with those of other more traditional therapeutic approaches. To facilitate clarity, evidence from each of these sources will be reviewed separately.

Anecdotal case and program reports

Despite their questionable value as sources of scientific evaluative data, certain case studies, program descriptions, and unsubstantiated statistical assertions have done much to bolster the current popular optimism regarding the efficacy of crisis intervention as psychotherapy. Among the more recent anecdotal claims made for it are the case studies reported by Kardener (1975) and Argles and Mackenzie (1970). Kardener describes crisis intervention as a "treatment modality of great value," one that offers therapists the opportunity to "exercise their enormous capacity to assist patients, effecting meaningful change in a brief time period." In support of his enthusiastic assertions, Kardener describes four cases in which crisis intervention was successfully used as psychotherapy. Argles and Mackenzie offer a lengthy and in-depth analysis of crisis intervention as a preferred psychotherapeutic modality for multi-problem families.

There is no question that the case study is a time-honored approach to many of the questions of concern to behavioral scientists and mental health professionals. As a tool for teaching psychotherapy or illustrating the clinical application of a specific modality, the case study may be invaluable. As a medium for the scientific evaluation of psychotherapy, however, its usefulness is generally minimal, by reason of obvious concern for selection bias, reliability, and generalizability.

It may be noted in defense of the case study approach that some behavior modification researchers outside the field of crisis intervention have made convincing use of single-subject research designs. These researchers, however, have taken care to exercise stringent controls over socio-environmental and other non-treatment variables, have employed multiple baselines in delineating pre-treatment functioning, and have made careful measures of change in client behavior over time. To date, case studies of crisis intervention have achieved no such methodological sophistication.

In addition to the case study, several investigators have relied upon what might be called program studies in an effort to document their claims for the efficacy of crisis intervention as psychotherapy. For example, Jacobson (1965), Chandler (1972), and Hoffman and Remmel (1975) have all offered accounts of crisis intervention programs, claiming "success" on the basis of data derived from questionable or unspecified measures.

Jacobson, for instance, describes a program of brief, immediately available psychotherapy utilizing the fundamental concepts of crisis intervention. By way of evaluation, he reports that approximately two-thirds of all clients treated in this program were considered "improved" by their therapists at termination. Not only does Jacobson make no mention of the criteria employed by therapists in making these judgments, but he readily acknowledges that such judgments provide no evidence regarding the "lastingness" of these improvements, nor any notion as to "what outcomes would be observed if a comparable group of patients were treated either not at all or in a different manner."

The obvious need for specification of criteria, post-treatment follow-up measures and the use of untreated or differently treated control clients is further emphasized by their absence in other anecdotal claims made for crisis intervention. As a case in point, Chandler, whose crisis intervention program was described in the preceding chapter, deems one program successful in that it apparently reduced the percentage of clients referred to a state hospital for treatment. Unfortunately, we have no way of knowing what criteria were used for referral to the state hospital, how these clients would have fared without crisis intervention or with some other form of treatment, or for how long they were actually kept from admission to the state hospital.

Hoffman and Remmel, whose program was also described in the last chapter, report finding that, at one year following treatment, clients who received crisis intervention were significantly more likely than those who received "traditional" psychotherapy to report improvement in their "marital-sexual" relationships and self-images. These authors, while apparently recognizing the need for long-term follow-up and at least some form of control group, not only fail to specify the nature of the treatment received by the "traditional" group, but also neglect any mention of sample size or criteria used to assess improvement. While their report does present methodological advances over those of Jacobson and Chandler, without more explicit description of methods and numbers, it too must be considered no more than anecdotal evidence for the efficacy of crisis intervention.

Uncontrolled outcome studies

By far the largest bulk of current evidence as to the efficacy of crisis intervention derives from a variety of studies, which, though more than simply anecdotal, fail to include any sort of control group, untreated or otherwise. Since crisis intervention seems most frequently used in child and/or family treatment settings, it is not surprising that most of these studies deal with children and their families.

Probably the most extensive study of this sort to date is that reported by Parad and Parad (1968). Surveying the records of ninety-eight child and family clinics offering "crisis-oriented planned short-term treatment," these investigators obtained data on the outcomes of 1,165 cases provided such treatment. Their data, based exclusively upon therapist's rating at termination, indicates that in 68.3 percent of these cases the "presenting problem" was "improved," in 63.1 percent the clients' "ability to cope with stress" was "improved," and in 36.1 percent the clients' "underlying personality problems" were "improved."

Shaw, Blumenfeld, and Senf (1968) also report similarly optimistic findings in another study of crisis intervention with child guidance cases. These investigators followed up 227 cases with interviews conducted twelve months after termination. Interviewers (who were mental health professionals) found 23.6 percent of the children and 16.82 percent of the parents "much improved," 32.5

percent of the children and 45 percent of the parents "moderately improved," and 43.9 percent of the children and 38.2 percent of the parents "unimproved."

Kaffman (1963), in a much smaller-scaled study, also found evidence of improvement among twenty-nine cases treated with family crisis intervention. In this study each case was rated for improvement by the therapist at termination. Therapist's ratings indicated "total symptomatic improvement" in ten cases, "considerable improvement" in eleven cases, and "moderate improvement" in four cases. Three cases were rated "unchanged" after treatment, and one case discontinued treatment before an evaluation could be made. Kaffman reports that these findings were essentially confirmed by a later follow-up conducted at six months after termination.

Wolkon (1972) looked at improvement among adult cases treated with crisis intervention. He reports that among sixty-four adult psychiatric clinic clients, forty-eight were rated by their therapists as being at least "moderately improved" at termination. Eleven of these forty-eight were rated "markedly improved." Wolkon, however, also reports on the outcomes of fourteen adult clients treated with crisis intervention in a sectarian family agency. Among these clients, only four were rated at least "moderately improved" at termination.

With the single exception of this last finding, the unanimous verdict of these studies is that crisis intervention is beneficial to the vast majority of clients who receive it. Unfortunately, however, none of these studies is capable of providing data sufficient to warrant such a judgment. Like most evaluative studies of psychotherapy, their methodologies in general are open to question, if not criticism, on a number of scores. The most telling criticism, though, involves their failure to include any sort of control group. Clearly, in the absence of some form of untreated control group, studies such as these cannot establish with any assurance that the "improvements" observed were, in fact, effects or products of the crisis intervention process. Such lack of control makes impossible any legitimate inference that factors other than the intervention could not reasonably have accounted for these "improvements" or that they would not have occurred anyway in the absence of treatment.

A controlled outcome study

In fairness to these researchers, it should be noted that the establishment, maintenance, and follow-up of adequate untreated control groups is an extremely difficult, often ethically questionable task. In general, evaluative studies of psychotherapy have for the most part failed to make use of such groups.

In the present context, however, it must also be noted that one study of crisis intervention has indeed included an untreated control group, representing a significant methodological milestone in the evaluation of this modality. Gottschalk, Fox, and Bates (1973) report having randomly assigned sixty-eight clients to one of two experimental conditions: 1. immediate crisis intervention, or 2. six-week waiting list for psychotherapy. Initially, all sixty-eight were evaluated on a number of psychological and psychiatric scales of adjustment. Six weeks later, prior to commencing treatment of the control group, each was again examined according to similar scales.

While Gottschalk and his colleagues are careful to qualify their findings in the light of various methodological limitations, essentially they found that over the six-week period the treated group had improved no more than the untreated group. As these investigators note, there is, of course, no way to be certain that clients in the untreated group did not receive some sort of intervention outside traditional psychiatric channels (e.g., counseling from friends or relatives) which might have accounted for some of the "considerable improvement" they showed. Yet these results, derived from what is perhaps the most methodologically sound and sophisticated study of its kind to date, must be viewed as seriously questioning much of the optimism generated by earlier uncontrolled studies of crisis intervention.

Comparative studies of outcome

A number of studies have purposefully avoided the practical and ethical difficulties involved in the establishment and follow-up of untreated control groups and have sought simply to compare the efficacy of crisis intervention to that of other psychotherapies. These comparative studies share with most of those already reviewed the as yet unverified assumption that crisis intervention is more effective than no intervention at all. They do, however, surpass the completely uncontrolled evaluations in usefulness, since for the most part they provide some evidence that even if crisis intervention is no more effective than no intervention, it is at least as effective as several other more traditional therapeutic approaches.

The prototype for studies comparing crisis intervention and other modalities lies in the research of Langsley, Kaplan, and their colleagues (Langsley and Kaplan, 1968; Langsley, Pittman, Machotka and Flomenhaft, 1968; Flomenhaft and Langsley, 1971). Langsley et al. randomly assigned 150 applicants for psychiatric hospitalization to outpatient family crisis intervention. Subsequently they compared this group of clients with another 150, all of whom were hospitalized upon application. Six- and eight-month follow-ups of these clients found that in terms of personal functioning, social adjustment, and family relations, the crisis intervention clients were at least as well off as those who had been hospitalized. On more objective measures, such as number and duration of subsequent hospitalizations and speed of return to employment, crisis intervention clients fared significantly better than the hospitalized clients at both six- and eighteen-month follow-ups.

These findings seem especially impressive from an economic

point of view, since treatment for the crisis intervention clients consisted of only five office visits, a home visit, and a few phone calls, whereas all control clients were hospitalized at a cost averaging 6.5 times that of family crisis intervention.

Decker and Stubblebine (1972) also have compared crisis intervention and hospitalization, and with similarly optimistic results. These investigators evaluated the post-treatment records of two groups of clients, both of whom had been hospitalized on psychiatric units of various institutions. One group $(N = 315)$ was routinely hospitalized and received "traditional modes of treatment" as inpatients. The other group $(N = 225)$ received crisis intervention treatment immediately prior to their hospitalization. Following the lives of these clients for two and one-half years after hospitalization, Decker and Stubblebine found that those who had first received crisis intervention spent significantly less time in the hospital (during both initial and subsequent hospitalizations) and were readmitted significantly fewer times than those who were routinely hospitalized. In addition, they found that six of the routinely hospitalized clients had subsequently committed suicide, whereas only one of the crisis intervention clients had done so.

Although the methods and measures utilized in this study might well be questioned, the investigation reported by Decker and Stubblebine seems particularly noteworthy in that, to the extent that hospitalization was roughly comparable for the two groups studied, in effect crisis intervention was compared with no treatment at all.

Two more recent studies have compared the efficacy of crisis intervention and that of traditional therapeutic approaches with children and families. In the first, Stratton (1975) sought to determine "whether family crisis intervention after initial police contact is more effective than the traditional methods of dealing with" predelinquent and misdemeanor juvenile offenders. Sixty youngsters, all of whom had been officially classified as belonging to one or the other of these legal categories, were randomly assigned to either traditional procedures or to family crisis-intervention services. The thirty cases in the traditional group received one of the following procedures: 1. informal counseling of juvenile and parents without arrest; 2. informal counseling followed by petition for family court action; or 3. immediate detention followed by court action within seventy-two hours of arrest.

Following up these cases for six months after their disposition, Stratton found that, on the average, juveniles in the traditional group committed more offenses, were rearrested and detained more frequently, and made greater use of further probation department services than those in the crisis intervention group. Only on the variable, total number of arrests, however, was there any *statistically significant* difference between the two groups.

In the other study Ewing (1975) compared family crisis intervention and traditional child guidance practice. Ewing randomly selected thirty family crisis intervention cases and thirty traditional child guidance cases from the closed case files of a mental health center for children and families. Families in the crisis intervention group had received an average of three and one-half hours of intensive family intervention based upon the principles of Caplan's crisis theory. Those in the traditional child guidance group had received an average of thirty-six and one-half hours treatment, including intake, diagnostic evaluation, and dynamically oriented psychotherapy.

Following up each case with a personal interview with the mother, conducted roughly seventeen months after termination, Ewing derived three measures of outcome: 1. percentage of abatement in child's symptoms; 2. change in child's adjustment; and 3. change in family's coping abilities (pretreatment to follow-up). On none of these measures was there a significant difference between the two groups of clients.

All these comparative studies adhere to a single basic research design (i.e., the follow-up comparison of two groups of clients, one treated with crisis intervention, the other with a more tradi-

VANDERBILT MEDICAL CENTER LIBRARY

tional approach). This design, though failing to demonstrate the *absolute* efficacy of crisis intervention as psychotherapy, allows for the demonstration of the *relative* efficacy of this modality. Given the belief of many if not most treatment facilities that clients must be treated somehow, this design, though not so powerful as the untreated control group design, seems likely to dominate future crisis intervention research. With this in mind, it may be valuable, before concluding the present discussion, to consider briefly some of the key methodological issues to be faced by future researchers operating within this limited framework.

The first two concerns in this regard relate to the need for adequate control of variables (other than treatment) that might affect significantly the outcome and thus bias comparisons. To begin with, researchers employing comparative designs such as those reviewed here must take pains to insure that client groups (however treated) are roughly comparable prior to treatment, especially in terms of variables such as age, sex, diagnosis, treatment history, and socio-familial status. Exact matching of clients across treatment groups is ordinarily impractical if not impossible. Random assignment of clients to treatments (as in the Langsley et al. and Stratton studies), though also sometimes unfeasible, is generally easier and often just as likely to reduce the chances of significant bias stemming from these and other client and clinical variables.

This issue is especially important in comparative studies involving crisis intervention. As has been noted in earlier chapters, crisis intervention is frequently provided to "all comers." Yet applicants for traditional treatments are usually screened to insure the likelihood of successful outcome. Thus, where crisis intervention and traditional approaches are compared in the absence of randomization or matching (as was the case in the Ewing and Decker studies), outcome measures will, in all probability, be biased significantly in favor of traditional treatments.

A related but often overlooked concern in studies of this sort involves the assignment of therapists. Numerous investigations

have indicated that therapist qualities—particularly experience—
may have significant bearing upon outcome in psychotherapy. This
issue is also important in crisis intervention studies, since (depending upon the setting) crisis therapists may ordinarily be more or
less experienced than therapists who provide other treatments. As
an example, the Framingham Youth Guidance Center, whose
Crisis Clinic is described in Chapter 5, uses only experienced staff
for crisis intervention, and both staff and trainees for traditional
child guidance treatment.

It would be difficult, if not impossible, to control the full range
of therapist variables that could conceivably affect outcome. Yet,
given the above described problem, it would seem essential that
future comparative studies involving crisis intervention make at
least some attempt to ensure that both crisis and traditional
groups are treated by therapists with roughly equal levels of experience.

In addition to these concerns, use of the comparative design requires careful consideration of a number of issues related to the
measurement of outcome. Actual measures to be used in studies
of this sort will of course depend upon the nature and goals of the
treatments compared—and crisis intervention researchers face a
special difficulty in this regard. The goals of crisis intervention,
though often ambitious, frequently fail to coincide with those of
other treatments, particularly those of long-term psychodynamic
approaches. Thus, comparative designs that utilize a single set of
criteria for assessing outcome may over- or under-estimate the
relative efficacy of crisis intervention. Yet designs which use different criteria for different treatments allow for no meaningful comparison.

As the present review indicates, researchers to date have ignored
this issue and have proceeded to use a single set of criteria in comparing crisis intervention and other approaches. There does seem
to be at least one potential solution to this dilemma, however: the
use of Goal Attainment Scaling (GAS), currently a popular tool

in evaluation research of all sorts. GAS, developed by Kiresuk and Sherman (1968), involves the establishment, prior to treatment, of an individualized set of goals for each client. These goals, generally set by someone other than the therapist, are established in such a way as to allow for the scaling of their attainment on a predetermined numerical scale ranging from +2 to o to −2 (+2 representing the most favorable outcome possible, o the expected outcome, and −2 the least favorable outcome for each goal).

Using GAS, each client's goal attainment can be assessed on this scale following treatment, and through a relatively simple statistical formula be transformed into standardized T-scores. As Kiresuk and Sherman have noted, when used in conjunction with random assignment of clients to treatment conditions, this method permits the "comparison of treatment modes within a program."

Two final measurement issues worth noting in the present context have to do with *when* and *by whom* the outcome should be assessed. Looking first to the latter issue, it would seem that the ego-involvement of most therapists and clients would eliminate them as unbiased judges of treatment outcome. Where GAS is used, its originators strongly suggest that independent raters be utilized to judge goal attainment. Ambitious researchers may wish to obtain ratings from several sources, including the therapist and client. But whatever measures of outcome are used, it would seem imperative that their assessment include ratings from at least one source not involved or invested in the treatments being compared.

As to *when* the outcome should be assessed, practical considerations such as the availability of clients for follow-up often have to be the ultimate determinant. Again, though, when one evaluates a treatment approach (such as crisis intervention) focusing only upon current conflicts and crises, the question of durability of treatment effects is especially significant. Thus, outcome measures in comparative studies involving this modality should be taken at periods long enough after termination to allow the investigator to determine whether its effects are as enduring as those of treatments with which it is compared. Where feasible, a multiple follow-up procedure (such as that used by Langsley et al.), extending over an eighteen-month period beyond termination, has many advantages and should be considered. In any event, adequate measurement in studies of this sort seems to demand assessment of outcome beyond any done simply at the time of termination.

Conclusion

Clearly, there is as yet no conclusive evidence regarding the efficacy or utility of crisis intervention as psychotherapy. As this review indicates, so far there have been only relatively few serious efforts to evaluate this modality, and most of these have been so thoroughly plagued with problems of control and other methodological difficulties as to preclude any unequivocal interpretation of their findings.

Yet these investigations, few in number and limited though they may be, should not go unappreciated. They have all been conducted and reported by concerned mental health professionals seeking useful data, generally under less than optimal research conditions imposed by the considerable constraints of time, money, and the realities and ethics of everyday clinical practice. If nothing else, the scientific curiosity of this group of clinician-researchers has helped break the ground and lay the foundation for the much needed evaluation of this popular but unproven approach to human problems.

Perhaps the value of such studies as well as the present state of crisis intervention research can best be summarized by quoting Jerome Frank, a pioneer in psychotherapy research. "What is most needed in research on psychotherapy," he has written,

> is originality of thought and courage to grapple with important issues, setting up as much control as feasible. Each experiment should lead to another which is an improvement over its predecessor. In this sense a bad experiment is better

than none, and several are better than one. Unless one makes the original crude experiments, no progress is possible. (1962, p. 25)

It can only be hoped that future investigators of crisis intervention will demonstrate such "originality" and "courage" in their efforts to build upon the works reviewed here.

7

Selecting appropriate clients
for crisis intervention

As was noted in Chapter 3, some clinicians have taken the position that anyone seeking mental health services is, *ipso facto*, in a state of crisis. But does this mean that every applicant for mental health services is thus a suitable client for crisis intervention? The purpose of this chapter is to explore the issue of *for whom*, and *under what circumstances*, crisis intervention may be an appropriate treatment choice.

Naturally, an almost infinite variety of factors may have bearing on this important issue. The focus of the present review, however, will be upon those client and clinical variables most frequently identified by mental health practitioners and researchers as significant in the decision to provide, or not to provide, crisis intervention as psychotherapy for a given client or client family. In the clinical and empirical literatures of psychology, psychiatry, and social work, some of these variables are: 1. duration of the client's problem(s); 2. severity of the problem(s); 3. diagnosis; 4. client's motivation for treatment; and 5. client's socio-economic status (SES). While it is recognized that such variables are almost always interrelated, if not interdependent, for the sake of clarity each will be considered separately here.

Duration of the problem(s)

Crisis theory, as described in Chapter 2, presupposes that crises are self-limiting and last for only a period of weeks. Thus, as was observed in Chapter 3, many clinicians feel that, to be effective, crisis intervention must be initiated as near as possible to the onset of the client's problems. Some practitioners have taken this interpretation even farther and have posited that crisis intervention can be applied successfully only in cases presenting problems of a relatively short duration. Kaplan (1968), for one, admonishes clinicians to "bear in mind that crisis intervention cannot solve all problems." Long-term, chronic problems, he cautions, "do exist and require traditional forms of intervention."

This notion—that duration of the client's problems may be a significant determinant of who will benefit most from crisis intervention—is supported by the findings of three outcome studies, those of Shaw et al. (1968), Waldfogel and Gardner (1961), and Wolkon (1972). In the study described in Chapter 6, Shaw and his colleagues found that among children with symptoms of less than a year's duration, 43 percent were rated "much improved" at follow-up. Among children with symptoms of greater than a year's duration, however, they found a "much improved" rate of only 18 percent.

Waldfogel and Gardner studied the relationship between duration of symptoms and outcome in crisis intervention with school-phobic children and their families. Among twenty-one children for whom the intervention was begun within the first semester of school absence, twenty returned to patterns of regular school attendance within three months, and fifteen of this number were back in school on a regular basis within three weeks. In five other cases, where the intervention began one or more semesters after onset of symptoms, none of the children treated established regular attendance during the three-month follow-up.

Wolkon, in a more recent study also reviewed in Chapter 6,

looked at the relation between time elapsed from application to initial interview and outcome among adult crisis-intervention clients. Combining psychiatric clinic and family-service agency clients, he found elapsed time related significantly to outcome: "The less the elapsed time between application and the first scheduled appointment, the greater the likelihood of improvement at termination of therapy." To the extent that Wolkon is correct in asserting that "the act of applying for help *per se* is a crisis," these findings may be viewed as supporting the position that duration of problem or crisis is indeed a significant factor to consider in assessing the likelihood that a client will benefit appreciably from crisis intervention.

In spite of its underpinning in crisis theory, however, this position regarding duration of the client's problem(s) is not universally regarded as valid. There is, in fact, both theory and evidence suggesting that duration of the problem has no significant bearing on the applicability or outcome of crisis intervention. Lang (1974), for instance, contends that clients "with chronic, entrenched pathology" can benefit from crisis intervention just as much as those with more acute difficulties. The findings of Parad and Parad (1968), Kaffman (1963) and Ewing (1975), all of whose studies were reviewed in Chapter 6, provide empirical support for this opposing position.

The Parads, in their study of 1165 child and family crisis intervention cases, report finding no significant association between outcome and time elapsed from onset of the client's problems to initiation of intervention. Kaffman reports that although all but five of the twenty-nine family crisis intervention cases he studied presented "chronic, well-established symptomatology," twenty-five of these cases achieved at least "moderate symptomatic improvement." Finally, Ewing reports that among the thirty crisis intervention cases he followed up, there were no significant outcome differences between those presenting "short-term problems" (less than six months' duration) and those presenting "long-term problems" (greater than six months' duration).

Obviously, there is to date no definitive answer to the question of whether crisis intervention should be regarded as contraindicated in cases presenting long-standing problems. Existing evidence is not only conflicting and dealing largely with only family and child cases, but allows for no judgment as to whether crisis intervention is more or less effective than any other modality in the treatment of long-term difficulties. In the absence of conclusive data, it can only be suggested that practitioners exercise common sense and critical clinical judgment in deciding whether or not to tackle long-term, sometimes chronic, problems with crisis intervention—a treatment approach designed in theory for relatively acute, short-standing conditions. In actual practice, the crisis intervention clinician will undoubtedly want to consider not only the duration but also the severity of the problem and the client's resources for dealing with it in determining the appropriateness of this modality.

Severity of the problem(s)

Duration of the client's problem is often directly related to the severity of that problem. It is difficult, however, to generalize about the nature of this relationship. Long-term problems, for instance, may be enduring because of their severity or because they are relatively non-serious and thus have not previously come to professional attention. By the same token, acute problems may be more or less serious than chronic difficulties, depending upon their impact upon the client and those around him.

Recognizing this, clinicians and researchers writing about crisis intervention have generally regarded duration and severity of problem as separate issues. One group (including Lang, 1974; Kaffman, 1963; and Chandler, 1972) seems to regard severity of the client's problem(s) as relatively unimportant in determining the suitability of a client for crisis intervention. Others (such as LaVietes, 1974, and Berlin, 1970), however, warn that clients with severe problems do not respond well to short-term therapies such as crisis intervention.

What little empirical evidence there is regarding this issue supports the judgment of this latter group of clinicians. The Parads (1968), for instance, report that among the crisis intervention cases they studied, those rated by therapists as presenting only a "moderate crisis" were much more likely than those rated as presenting a "severe crisis" to show improvement at termination. Ewing (1975) reports that among the family crisis-intervention cases he followed up, those in which the clients described their presenting problems as no more than "moderately serious" had significantly more favorable outcomes than those in which clients described their presenting problems as "very serious" or "extremely serious." Perhaps even more importantly, he found that among clients with "very" or "extremely serious" problems, those who received traditional long-term treatment had significantly more favorable outcomes than those who received crisis intervention.

Clearly, these two studies provide only relatively little evidence. Yet their findings are consistent and must be viewed as suggesting that severity of the problem is indeed an issue worthy of consideration in the decision to offer, or not to offer, crisis intervention to a given client. Ideally, future research in this area should seek to specify particular indices of severity that may have relevance for crisis intervention practice.

In view of the present evidence on this issue, it would seem important that clinicians exercise considerable caution in regarding crisis intervention as a treatment of choice for cases presenting rather serious problems. Where clients present problems that are both rather serious and of a chronic or long-standing nature, even greater caution would seem indicated.

Diagnosis

Related to and yet separate from duration and severity of the client's problem is the issue of diagnosis. Traditionally, mental health professionals have viewed careful diagnosis as a fundamental and necessary antecedent to effective treatment. In recent years, however, this view has come under increased opposition and criticism. In fact, disenchantment with psychiatric diagnostic concepts has become so great in certain quarters that clinicians have taken the radical position that diagnosis *per se* is no longer relevant to the task of providing adequate mental health treatment.

The greatest support for this stance has come, in most recent times, from behaviorally oriented clinicians. These workers, of course, reject the traditional medical model of psychopathology and view psychological disorders not as illnesses to be diagnosed but rather as learned maladaptive responses to be unlearned. As might be expected, however, given their crisis theory orientation (which similarly rejects the medical or illness model), crisis intervention advocates have also lent much support to this radical position

Lang (1974), for instance, suggests the "pragmatic stance" that "suitability" of clients for crisis intervention "has more to do with worker expectations and goals than with diagnostic categories." Kaffman (1963) notes that in the clinic he studied, "suitable cases" for crisis intervention "embraced all forms of psychopathology." And, as mentioned in Chapter 5, Chandler (1972) has asserted that "diagnosis" is "irrelevant" in the "decision to provide outpatient crisis intervention in preference to other dispositions." More recently, it has even been suggested that far from being essential, diagnosis may have a negative impact on crisis intervention practice. Butcher and Maudal (1976), for example, warn that

> Formal psychiatric diagnosis is not particularly useful in crisis therapy and may in fact be detrimental, in that it may orient

the therapist toward seeing and planning for "chronic pathology" and blind him to important and manageable critical events. (P. 618)

Does diagnosis really make any difference in crisis intervention? Unfortunately, there is very little empirical evidence bearing directly on this question. The effect of diagnosis on the *process* of crisis intervention has apparently never been given systematic empirical attention. The effect of diagnosis on the *outcome* of crisis intervention has been considered in two studies, both dealing with child and family treatment.

In the first study, Shaw et al. (1968) found that families with neurotic children showed much greater "improvement" than those with children diagnosed as behavior or character disorders. Indeed, these investigators report finding that at a one-year follow-up, the majority (56.4 percent) of these latter families were "unimproved." In the more recent study, however, Ewing (1975) found no significant outcome differences between family crisis intervention cases in which the child's diagnosis was either neurosis or adjustment reaction of childhood and those in which the diagnosis was one of behavioral or personality disorder.

Unfortunately, these data are not only conflicting and limited to child and family cases; they also offer no assessment of the merits of crisis intervention in the treatment of clients with more debilitating diagnoses, such as those applied to the psychotic-level thought and mood disorders. Nor do these data offer any insight into the effect of diagnosis on the process of crisis intervention or any indication as to how crisis intervention compares with alternative modalities in the treatment of various diagnostic groups.

Clearly, diagnosis is an open issue that deserves further empirical attention from crisis intervention practitioners and researchers. For the moment, clinicians have only their own judgment to rely upon in assessing the need for and the role of diagnosis in determining the appropriateness of crisis intervention for their clients. Those who choose to eschew diagnosis, however, should be reminded that diagnosis and assessment are not synonymous. While formal diagnostic procedures may be of questionable value, as Butcher and Maudal (1976) observe, "the importance of assessment in crisis work cannot be overemphasized." It is difficult to disagree with these authors' contention that, regardless of the role of formal diagnosis, crisis intervention must include at least an adequate assessment of the client's 1. current level of functioning; 2. emotional state; 3. pre-morbid adjustment; 4. manner of relating; 5. current life stresses; and 6. level of motivation for treatment.

Motivation for treatment

This last area to be assessed—client's motivation for treatment—is singled out for consideration because of the extremely high premium placed upon motivation by psychotherapists, regardless of their theoretical orientations. Meltzoff and Kornreich (1970), for example, have asserted that "one of the axioms of psychotherapy is that an individual has to be motivated for it and want to change if any change is to take place." Rexford (1959) elaborates this assertion, observing that

> A basic assumption of psychotherapy and casework is that an individual is willing and able to take responsibility to try to find out what the trouble is, to think about it, to try to change not only his actions but his attitudes. (P. 18)

A like importance is attached to motivation by crisis intervention therapists, although some apparently take it for granted that their clients are motivated to change. As mentioned in Chapter 3, numerous crisis-intervention practitioners have identified any request for mental health services as a crisis. Since crisis theory (see Chapter 2) maintains that one in crisis is likely to turn to others for help and at the same time be more susceptible to that help, some clinicians seem to assume motivation on the part of crisis intervention clients. Kaplan (1968), for instance, has argued that a client's motivation for help and change is "generally strong" during crisis because his "personal distress" is "unusually high."

Motivation for help and change, however, even during crisis, is not always what therapists would desire it to be. Many clients, though greatly distressed by their situations, seek professional help only at the insistence of some external source of authority (e.g., employer, school, family physician, court). The issue of motivation is especially significant to crisis intervention practitioners for at least two reasons. First, the short-term, time-limited nature of crisis intervention precludes the extensive working-through of client resistance, often regarded as an essential part of long-term psychotherapy efforts. And secondly, of course, by virtue of its emphasis on family and social networks (see Chapter 3), crisis intervention must consider not only the motivation of the "nominal client," but also that of other family members, who may or may not share the client's enthusiasm for help and change. Not infrequently the therapist may meet with cases in which a family is seriously divided over the question of whether or not to pursue treatment.

Empirically, there is a good deal of evidence to suggest that motivation for treatment may indeed be a significant determinant of success in crisis intervention. Shaw et al. (1968), for instance, found in their follow-up of family crisis intervention cases that both mother and child's "motivation for treatment" was significantly related to improvement. The studies of Kaffman (1963) and Ewing (1975) have yielded similar findings: positive motivation for treatment is significantly associated with marked improvement in crisis intervention cases. Additionally, Cowan, Currie, Krol, and Richardson (1969) have presented case material leading to their conclusion that crisis intervention is not a viable approach to psychotherapy with "unwilling" families.

Clinically, it is often difficult to assess accurately client motivation for treatment. And where whole families are to be included in the treatment process, this difficulty is compounded. Ewing

(1975) has suggested that the extent to which clients voice approval of the referral source and the extent to which family members are united in the decision to seek outside help may have particular value as indices of motivation in family crisis intervention. Butcher and Maudal (1976) have noted that the question of what actions the clients have taken prior to treatment to resolve their problems may also be significant in this regard.

Whatever means are used, however, present evidence indicates that the clinician would do well to assess carefully his clients' motivation for treatment and change and explore alternatives to crisis intervention in cases where such motivation is lacking.

Socio-economic status (SES)

An enduring controversy in the mental health field has centered on the best way to meet the treatment needs of the poor and the disadvantaged. In the present context it is important to note that a number of clinicians have asserted that short-term, highly focused treatment such as crisis intervention may be the most appropriate way to meet the challenge posed by such clients.

Duckworth (1967), for example, suggests that among lower SES clients, crisis intervention is more likely than "usual" psychotherapeutic modalities to resolve emotional problems. Weinberger (1971) contends that the prevailing model of psychiatric treatment—at least that for child and family problems—is appropriate and relevant for only 5 to 10 percent of all clients, the brightest, most verbal, and "well-to-do." The remainder (i.e., the vast majority of clients), he says, will fare much better with short-term, problem-focused, pragmatic family treatment such as crisis intervention.

Kaffman (1963) concurs with these positions and suggests a rationale for them in terms of cross-class differences in expectations. Stating that much of the outcome in mental health treatment is determined by shared expectations between client and therapist, Kaffman concludes that short-term therapy such as crisis intervention is the treatment of choice for clients from the lower social classes. According to Kaffman, the lower SES client is less likely than his middle- or upper-class counterpart to understand the need for long-term treatment: rather, he often expects rapid solutions and frequently becomes "suspicious and uncooperative" if long-term treatment is mentioned or recommended. By the same token, Kaffman asserts, the more sophisticated middle- or upper-class client may become skeptical, disappointed, or even uncooperative if short-term treatment is offered.

While prevailing opinion appears to regard crisis intervention as a suitable and appropriate treatment mode for lower SES clients, at least some concern has been expressed regarding its suitability for clients with unusually deprived and disadvantaged backgrounds. Berlin (1970) has cautioned that clients "who have very primitive styles of living" or who "have had few gratifications in their infancy and childhood" do not respond well to crisis intervention. And Cowan and her colleagues (1968) have warned that

> The current emphasis on short-term counseling and crisis intervention may result in the provision of more effective service to more individuals, but severely deprived families cannot benefit significantly from such an approach. (P. 151)

Unfortunately, there is very little empirical data bearing directly upon the relation between SES and outcome in crisis intervention. When Ewing (1975) considered this issue, he found no significant relation between SES and outcome in the family crisis intervention cases he studied—but then his sample included only two families from the very lowest socio-economic level.

In all, the question of SES remains a difficult one for crisis intervention practitioners. Especially troublesome to these clinicians is the problem of how best to treat clients from particularly deprived and low socio-economic backgrounds, clients whose lives are a series of crises. Where the only alternatives are short-term crisis intervention and long-term dynamic psychotherapy, the choice may be relatively simple. Crisis intervention will probably be more in keeping with the client's expectations and thus will be the better of the two alternatives.

As LaVietes (1974) suggests, however, what these clients probably really need is a third alternative, a treatment approach offering relevant advantages of both crisis intervention and long-term traditional treatment. One is hard-pressed to argue with her conclusion that any viable treatment approach to the mental health problems of "ghetto" clients must include:

1. A spectrum of interventions that will vary from time to time, ranging from the concrete to the insightful.

2. A long-term association with a helping agent, which will at times be intensive and at other times minimal.

3. An advocate for the child's and family's rights to emotional and physical well-being.

4. Access to highly skilled specialists as needed.

5. An executive agent to help them negotiate with what may appear to be a hostile or mysterious system: the welfare department, the school, the hospital, the court, etc.

6. A flexible approach to type, location and timing of service. (P. 720)

Conclusion

As this chapter has indicated, the issue of *for whom* and *under what circumstances* crisis intervention is a viable and appropriate treatment choice remains controversial. At present it is impossible to suggest any hard-and-fast criteria for use in selecting suitable clients for crisis intervention. Of the variables discussed here, severity of the client's problem, his motivation for treatment, and his socio-economic standing are perhaps the most significant features to be considered by the crisis therapist.

Future research and clinical experience with crisis techniques will undoubtedly shed additional light on the significance of these and other client and clinical variables. For the moment, however, careful assessment, sound clinical judgment, and common sense remain the clinician's best tools for determining who should and who should not receive crisis intervention.

8

The future of crisis intervention

The intent of the preceding chapters has been to provide a survey of the development and current status of crisis intervention as psychotherapy, and to offer an introduction to the theoretical and clinical concepts that guide its use, a description of the wide variety of ways in which it is used in clinical settings, and a review of current evidence regarding its efficacy and applicability as a psychotherapeutic modality.

As these chapters have indicated, thus far crisis intervention appears to be an innovative and evolving approach to mental health problems, growing in popularity and utilization among practicing professionals. But will crisis intervention continue to grow in use and acceptance and secure for itself a lasting place among the "tools" of the mental health professional? Or, as Specter and Claiborn (1973) ask, will it "join moral therapy, insulin shock therapy, and psychosurgery as an approach which had its day and then largely disappeared?" The purpose of this chapter is to explore a number of issues that may be significant in determining the future of crisis intervention as psychotherapy.

Crisis intervention and the medical model

The medical or illness model of psychological dysfunction is by far the most popular theoretical approach to the understanding and treatment of mental health problems. While the boundaries of professional practice have been expanding in recent years to include a variety of approaches to such problems, it is clear that the vast majority of mental health treatment programs remain dominated by this powerful traditional model. This theoretical bias, especially common among medically trained clinicians who often hold key positions in the mental health hierarchy, undoubtedly has been and may continue to be an obstacle to the full acceptance and greater use of crisis intervention as psychotherapy.

As mentioned briefly in Chapter 7, crisis theory (the theoretical foundation for crisis intervention practice) stands in direct conflict with the medical or illness perspective. There are many variations of the medical model, but essentially it regards disturbances in psychological functioning as manifestations of underlying biological or characterological defects (broadly characterized as "mental illnesses"). The logical consequence of adherence to this model has been the widespread development and use of clinical procedures aimed at determining the nature of (i.e., *diagnosing*), altering the presumed pathological effects of (i.e., *treating*), and where possible ridding the individual of (i.e., *curing*) these defects.

In contrast, crisis theory regards most disturbances of psychological functioning as the result not of underlying personal defects but rather of a temporary inability to cope adaptively with overwhelming life stresses. Approached from this perspective, psychological distress is seen not as symptomatic of illness but as a normal, predictable consequence of a stress-induced upset in the pattern and balance of emotional functioning. As earlier chapters indicate, adoption of this model has led to clinical procedures, not for the diagnosis and treatment of "mental illness," but rather for helping the individual (and/or family) to minimize the disorganizing impact of current stresses while developing stronger, more effective coping mechanisms. As has been indicated, the goal of these procedures is not to "cure" the client but rather to restore him to at least his usual (pre-crisis) level of psychological functioning. While crisis theory allows that "crises" may lead to psychopathology, one of its essential tenets is that with appropriate and timely intervention, they may just as likely lead to improved psychological functioning.

Table 1 summarizes the key differences between the medical and crisis models. As can be seen in the table, these models dictate not only different problems (or professional domains) but also different aims, methods, and ultimate goals.

Table 1
Crisis theory and the medical model

	Crisis theory	Medical model
PROBLEM	"Crises" (emotional reactions to situations in which normal adaptive coping mechanisms are overtaxed by overwhelming life stresses).	"Mental illnesses" (underlying biological or characterological defects which result in manifest symptomatology).
AIM	Help individual experiencing crisis cope more effectively with current stresses and develop greater capacity for future coping.	Diagnose and treat underlying illness.
METHODS	Short-term crisis intervention (see Chapter 3).	Traditional psychiatric diagnostic and treatment procedures (diagnostic interviews and/or testing, dynamic psychotherapy, hospitalization, psychotropic medication, electroconvulsive therapy, etc.).
GOAL	Restore individual to pre-crisis level of functioning and render him less vulnerable to future stresses.	Cure illness and restore individual to a state of "mental health."

In the present eclectic age, of course, only the most dogmatic practitioners adhere to models such as these in their "pure" forms. Although a number of clinicians do subscribe to a single theoretical approach, most allow experience and judgment to modify their interpretations and clinical applications of that approach. The differences between the crisis and medical models, however, may be so fundamental that many clinicians, particularly those trained and/or working in medical settings, may be unable or unwilling ever to embrace fully the concepts and practices of crisis intervention. Certainly, acceptance and use of crisis intervention by many such professionals would require not only radical modification of some of their basic assumptions about the nature and treatment of psychological disorders, but also the development of a new repertoire of clinical skills and an alteration in their traditional (often highly revered) professional roles (see Chapter 3, section 7).

Naturally, it is impossible to predict exactly how much this theoretical opposition will inhibit future acceptance and utilization of crisis intervention as psychotherapy. There is, however, reason to believe that the inhibiting impact of the medical model may be considerably less than might be expected. First of all, as this volume attests, the number of clinicians and programs committed to crisis intervention, in one form or another, is increasing substantially. Significantly, a growing number of these clinicians are psychiatrists, the most medically-oriented of all mental health practitioners. In many cases these physicians are not only practicing crisis intervention but are also making significant contributions to its understanding and acceptance (see, for example, Berlin, 1970; Langsley et al., 1968, and 1972; Chandler, 1972; Schwartz, 1971; Gottschalk et al., 1973; Bartolucci and Drayer, 1973; Hankoff et al., 1974; and Kardener, 1975).

Moreover, even within traditionally medical facilities, commitment to the crisis approach seems to be steadily growing. As pointed out in earlier chapters, numerous mental hospitals, psychiatric clinics, and even general-hospital emergency rooms have instituted crisis intervention programs.

Finally, and perhaps most significantly, there is growing reason to believe that, regardless of theoretical biases, clinicians everywhere are, out of necessity if not conviction, adjusting their psychotherapeutic practices in directions congruent with if not dictated by crisis theory. Client and community demands for immediate service are leading to the wholesale abandonment of waiting lists in many agencies. Economic pressure from health insurers and other third-party payment sources is rapidly spelling an end to long-term mental health treatment. And the ever-growing demand for accountability (i.e., demonstrable treatment results) is forcing a major shift in psychotherapeutic practice toward more highly focused treatment of clearly specified problems.

Obviously, trends such as these cannot be read as spelling doom for the influential medical model of understanding and treating mental health problems. Nor can they be viewed as foreshadowing the ultimate domination of mental health services by the crisis approach. They must be interpreted, however, as suggesting that the future of psychotherapy will be dictated less by ideology than by practical, economic necessity. Given such an interpretation, one cannot help but speculate that while theoretical opposition to crisis intervention may continue, its significance as an obstacle to greater utilization of this modality can be expected to diminish sharply.

Crisis intervention and mental health service delivery systems

In addition to theoretical opposition, crisis intervention is also faced with a number of obstacles associated with contemporary models for the delivery of mental health services. Outpatient mental health services in the United States today are delivered largely by either private practitioners or publicly supported clinics, usually designated as community mental health centers. The organization of mental health care around these two types of delivery systems has had and will probably continue to have important implications for the utilization of crisis intervention as psychotherapy.

To look first to the private practice of psychotherapy: it is clear that several factors hinder extensive utilization of crisis intervention. To begin with, the economic realities of independent "fee-for-service" practice are such that the practitioner must maintain a relatively stable caseload if he is to ensure his livelihood. The most practical way to maintain such stability, of course, is to make long-term treatment contracts with clients. Now, some private therapists do offer short-term treatment (this is especially true of psychiatrists with a large practice). But unless the clinician has a consistently steady influx of new clients, short-term modalities such as crisis intervention will probably not be economically feasible.

In addition, many clinicians in private, independent practice may avoid doing crisis work because it is emotionally so demanding. As Sebolt (1973) observes,

> Because of its very intense nature . . . the crisis approach can be anxiety-provoking for the therapist. . . . A steady diet of crisis cases with no outlet for affectively dealing with such feelings often results in a crisis therapist himself being in crisis. (P. 73)

Both Sebolt and Ewalt and Cohen (1971) have observed that crisis therapists frequently require a good deal of emotional support from their colleagues, and that, further, in a clinic setting, emotional "backup" of this kind may be provided by organizing crisis intervention clinicians into teams, the members of which meet frequently to share feelings, confront, comfort, and support one another. The independent practitioner, for his part, usually has no such ready outlet for his emotions.

Although these are very real barriers to the use of crisis intervention as psychotherapy in private practice, there are reasons for believing that mental health providers in the private sector may, in the future, become much more open to the use of this modality. First of all (as mentioned earlier in this chapter), health insurers and other third-party payment sources, though perhaps encouraging the use of private therapists, are pressing for an end to costly long-term mental health treatment. Thus, private practitioners whose clients rely heavily upon insurance or other reimbursement for fees may be forced to move toward short-term treatment approaches such as crisis intervention.

Perhaps more significant, however, is the growing trend in private health care toward concepts of group and/or prepaid practice. In a group mental-health practice consisting of several clinicians, crisis intervention should be much more feasible than in independent private practice in which the clinician is on his own both economically as well as emotionally.

There are few, if any, prepaid practices offering only mental health services. Yet there is a growing number of prepaid practices (sometimes designated as health maintenance organizations) which, even though primarily concerned with physical health, do offer mental health treatment. An often stated goal (if not an economic necessity) of such practices is the prevention of serious, costly illnesses among subscribers. Thus, it is not surprising that Federal regulations require health maintenance organizations to include among subscriber benefits:

> At least 20 outpatient visits per year, as may be necessary and appropriate, for short-term evaluative or crisis intervention services or both. (Public Health Title 42; Subchapter J; Section 110.102)

Whether or not health maintenance organizations interpret this regulation as requiring the kind of crisis intervention services described in this volume remains to be seen. In any event, however, the continued development of such organizations and similar group practices under Federal regulation seems likely to be an important factor in moving private mental-health service delivery in directions favorable to the acceptance and utilization of crisis intervention concepts.

The organization and delivery of outpatient mental health services in the *public* sector, i.e., through government-supported community-based clinics, offers great opportunity for the widespread utilization of crisis intervention as psychotherapy. Federally financed community mental health centers (CMHC's) were designed with the notion that early detection and treatment of emotional problems can help keep troubled people out of the hospital and in the community. They are legally mandated to provide emergency mental health services to persons in crisis. Indeed, a recent survey of CMHC's (National Institute of Mental Health Statistical Note 128, 1976) found that 76 percent offered immediate services on a 24-hour a day basis.

Given their theoretical rationale and obvious emphasis on immediately available services, CMHC's should be expected to provide significant impetus to the utilization of the crisis approach. There is, however, reason to believe that CMHC's for the most part have not made extensive use of crisis intervention (at least as it has been described in this volume). Statistics such as those of NIMH described above, while indicating the widespread availability of immediate mental health services to those in crisis, cannot be taken as accurate, reliable indicators of the extent to which crisis intervention is being used as a CMHC treatment modality.

Certainly there are CMHC's utilizing crisis intervention as psychotherapy. The bulk of CMHC immediate services, however, are oriented toward emergency evaluation or triage rather than crisis intervention. These services, though sometimes advertised as crisis intervention, often amount only to brief evaluation followed by discharge or referral to traditional services such as hospitalization or outpatient evaluation/treatment. Thus, they serve as a means for *screening* rather than actually *treating* clients.

As Beigel and Levenson (1972) observe, this screening and referral function is in itself an important and often essential aspect of CMHC emergency services. But, as they also note, if CMHC emergency personnel are trained in and encouraged to use crisis intervention, "then the definitive care for many patients can be handled within the emergency service, and referral is not needed." In the long run, much of the future of crisis intervention as psychotherapy may rest upon the extent to which CMHC administrators and clinicians accept this suggestion and utilize crisis intervention as a primary treatment modality.

Crisis intervention and the question of lay therapists

The present volume has been addressed exclusively to a consideration of crisis intervention as a *professional* enterprise, a form of psychotherapy conducted by highly trained and qualified clinicians. Yet there is a growing trend toward the use of paraprofessionals and non-professionals as crisis intervention therapists. Thus, in assessing the future of crisis intervention as psychotherapy, there is a need to consider the implications of this trend.

The most immediate implication has been the division of professional crisis-intervention clinicians into two "warring" factions. On one hand, there are professionals who welcome and encourage the use of laymen as crisis intervention therapists. Butcher and Maudal (1976), for example, assert that the problems of many clients are such that they "do not require the attention of highly specialized psychotherapists with advanced degrees." Many of these clients, they argue, "may be handled adroitly by an informed and attentive lay person."

Others such as Specter and Claiborn (1973) feel that, largely because they are *not* professionals, laymen may be uniquely qualified as crisis therapists. As they observe,

It may be yet that the enthusiasm, lack of theoretical bias, and lesser role conflict of the non-professional actually give him advantages over the professional worker. (P. 49)

On the other hand, many mental health professionals are clearly disturbed by this trend. McColskey (1973), for instance, sees "no justification" for the use of laymen as crisis therapists and observes that their use as such "is as illogical and hazardous as attempting to stem a massive hemorrhage with a band-aid."

This controversy, regardless of its ultimate resolution, may in itself have considerable impact on the future of crisis intervention. It may, for instance, lead to further assessment and evaluation of crisis intervention and to more serious attempts to clarify its nature and applicability. Or, less optimistically, it may "heat up" to the point where so much energy is lost on "infighting" that more vital substantive issues are neglected.

The long-range implications of the lay trend, of course, will depend largely upon the extent to which non-professionals prove capable as crisis interventionists. Increased lay participation in *successful* crisis intervention programs can only serve to increase acceptance and utilization of this modality. There remains at present, however, the persistent fear that lay therapists, for want of experience and expertise, will undermine the value of crisis intervention to clients, give the modality a "bad name" among professionals, and thus reduce both acceptance and utilization.

Crisis intervention and evaluative research

A final issue worth considering at least briefly relates to the role that evaluative research may play in determining the future of crisis intervention as psychotherapy. As was observed in Chapter 6, crisis intervention has generated great enthusiasm and optimism among its practitioners, but there is as yet no conclusive evidence that it is effective. To what extent, if any, will research evidence or the lack of it affect the future of crisis intervention?

There are some (such as Pasewark and Albers, 1972) who contend that the lack of conclusive evidence as to its efficacy has greatly limited acceptance and utilization of crisis intervention on the part of mental health professionals. While there is growing demand for evaluation and accountability in mental health work, there is thus far little reason to believe that evaluative research has had much actual impact on the practice of psychotherapy. To date there is little if any scientifically conclusive evidence that any form of psychotherapy is truly effective—indeed, in many cases, there is good reason to believe that psychotherapy may be no more helpful than the mere passage of time. Yet the practice of psychotherapy continues to grow and flourish.

There is no doubt that substantial positive research findings may enhance future acceptance and utilization of crisis intervention as psychotherapy. In the long run, however, it seems unlikely that evaluative research or the lack of it will "make or break" crisis intervention or any other psychotherapeutic approach. More likely, such research will lead to refinements in clinical procedures and to a better understanding of the applicability of crisis intervention.

A final note

In spite of some very real obstacles such as those outlined in this chapter, the future of crisis intervention appears bright. In this age of fiscal "belt-tightening" and growing demand for quality mental health care, crisis intervention offers a fresh, economical, and often highly effective alternative to costly, traditional long-term psychotherapeutic approaches. As has been noted above, crisis intervention is not suitable for *every* client; yet when used skillfully, it seems likely to meet the pressing mental health needs of many, some of whom might otherwise never be served.

Ultimately, of course, the future of crisis intervention will be determined by the interaction of multiple factors, both practical and theoretical. Perhaps the most important factor, however, will be the extent to which its principles and practices are understood by those concerned with and committed to improving the mental health and emotional well-being of their fellow man. It is hoped that, in at least some small measure, the present volume has increased this understanding and thus contributed to the future of crisis intervention as psychotherapy.

II

A model for the clinical practice
of crisis intervention as psychotherapy

Like any form of psychotherapy, crisis intervention is best learned through actual clinical experience, under the guidance and supervision of experienced clinicians. The training of psychotherapists has been and continues to be essentially a form of apprenticeship in which the novice therapist develops clinical skills "on the job." This being so, relatively few written works purport to "teach" new clinicians how to "do" psychotherapy.

The present volume was not intended to be an exception in this regard. Indeed, the author is firmly committed to the notion that, in developing psychotherapeutic skills, there is no substitute for extensive supervised clinical experience. Yet, in discussing a form of psychotherapy such as crisis intervention, about which there is so much confusion even among experienced clinicians, there is a pressing need (particularly among beginning-level therapists) for at least a minimal model or set of guidelines for clinical practice.

Accordingly, this section offers the interested reader an introductory (though by no means comprehensive) working model for the clinical practice of crisis intervention as psychotherapy. In pursuing this purpose, a preliminary warning may be in order—to-wit: The experienced mental health professional may find little that is new here. The model to be presented draws upon many well-known, frequently used principles, tactics, and procedures, some of which are fundamental to most psychotherapeutic approaches.

It is hoped, nevertheless, that even experienced clinicians may find the model proposed here useful in furthering their understanding of crisis intervention as a psychotherapeutic modality. Experienced clinicians (whether practicing crisis intervention or not) may be interested in examining the ways in which this model parallels—and diverges from—their own approaches. In addition, such clinicians may find this model useful in their roles as teachers or clinical supervisors of beginning-level therapists with an interest in crisis-oriented treatment.

Naturally, it is expected that the novice or student therapist will be the chief beneficiary of the proposed model, and that it may provide a clinical basis upon which such therapist may build in his own actual work with clients. The student or trainee is cautioned, however, to bear in mind that what will be presented here is only a *general* model, applicable in practice only insofar as it may be modified to meet the individual and unique needs of specific clients. As has been stressed at various points in this volume, pragmatism and flexibility are crucial elements in effective crisis intervention. Thus, the novice crisis therapist would do well to keep an open mind and regard the present model as suggestive only: as perhaps a good place to begin but in no way the final word.

As this volume has indicated, crisis intervention has been conceptualized as a psychotherapeutic modality in numerous ways. For present purposes, however, crisis intervention may be viewed as encompassing six essential stages: 1. Delineating the problem-focus; 2. Evaluation; 3. Contracting; 4. Intervening; 5. Termination; and 6. Follow-up. While for practical purposes each of these "stages" will be treated separately and as though they were sequential, in actual practice certain of them may overlap and converge frequently throughout the therapeutic process.

Delineating the problem-focus

As has been emphasized throughout this volume, crisis intervention is a brief and highly focused treatment modality. Because such a relatively small amount of time is involved, crisis therapists and their clients must work together quickly to define a fairly specific problem area toward which the intervention may be directed. Most practicing crisis therapists agree that without a clearly defined problem-focus, effective crisis intervention cannot proceed.

Occasionally the therapist will meet a client who can, with very little help, quickly and clearly articulate a highly specific problem (or a set of related problems) that may be considered an appropriate focus for crisis intervention. Such cases, however, tend to be more the exception than the rule. More often, the therapist is confronted with clients presenting multiple difficulties or having only very vague ideas about what is troubling them. Not infrequently, too, the therapist is faced with clients who, for reasons conscious or unconscious, avoid recognition or mention of their real concerns. Thus, in approaching what is perhaps the "typical" client, the crisis therapist must expect to devote considerable energy to exploring the client's problems in some detail before arriving at any specific focus for intervention.

Obviously, the most useful approach to delineating the problem-focus will be questioning or otherwise encouraging the client to tell the therapist why he is seeking treatment at this time. The crisis therapist, however, must be especially careful not to move too quickly at this stage. Though time is clearly limited, the therapist must bear in mind that the client, in seeking treatment, may be approaching a totally new and unfamiliar situation. More than likely, though harboring at least some expectation of being helped, the client is distraught, apprehensive, uncertain of himself, and perhaps even somewhat distrustful of the therapist. In addition, the client may be ashamed, fearful of being labeled "mentally ill," and afraid of being rejected by the therapist. Before much meaningful clinical inquiry can occur, feelings such as these must be taken into account and the client put at ease. This process, often referred to as developing rapport with the client, is a vital and time-consuming aspect of virtually all psychotherapy. In crisis intervention, even though time is short, it is necessarily the first order of business.

How does the crisis therapist develop rapport with the client in a very short time? Surely a good part of the answer to this question lies in the therapist's own personality makeup and functioning. Although one need not be a paragon of "mental health" to be a successful crisis therapist, personal virtues such as warmth, caring, empathy, and self-confidence go a long way, by themselves, toward encouraging openness and trust between client and therapist.

Aside from these personal qualities—and more specific to the practice of crisis intervention—the crisis therapist encourages rapport through words and actions designed to put the client at ease. The therapist, for example, opens treatment by introducing himself and briefly explaining the nature of the services available to the client. While the phrase "crisis intervention" probably will not be used, it is often helpful to describe the treatment approach to the client in crisis-oriented terms. The actual situation dictates what is said in this regard, but the client may be told something such as:

> As you may already know, we generally see people here on a short-term basis only. We feel that most people who come in for help are not mentally ill, but simply have problems they can't cope with right at the moment. Our major concern is to help get things going smoothly again as quickly as possible. I'll be available to meet with you (and your family) for up to X hours over the next few weeks, if you feel that would be

helpful. A little help at the right time is what most people seem to need, but if later you decide that you want more help than this, I may be able to help arrange that, too.

A message such as this, if conveyed with sincerity, says a great deal to the client. It lets most clients know that they will not be viewed as mentally ill or rejected by the therapist, that they can expect help quickly and without an inordinate investment of time, and that the therapist is interested in them and optimistic that they can be helped. Such a message does not automatically lead to what some have called "instant rapport." Yet when coupled with honest, caring concern for the client's feelings and reservations about treatment, it should help to establish the kind of client-therapist relation needed before meaningful attempts at delineating a problem-focus can be made.

As was suggested earlier in this volume, perhaps the easiest way to begin the search for an appropriate problem-focus is to ask the client (in a number of ways), "Why *now?*" or "What has led you to seek treatment at this particular time?" Some clients have recently experienced a highly traumatic event (e.g., rape, loss of livelihood, or death of a loved one). The overwhelming nature of such an event often dictates the problem-focus, and thus the intervention may be directed quickly toward enabling the client to understand the trauma, cope effectively with it, and return to emotional equilibrium.

Many (if not most) clients, however, present no such clearly identifiable trauma. Indeed, many clients present only "symptoms" (e.g., anxiety, insomnia, impaired interpersonal and/or sexual functioning, vague feelings of impending disaster, unexplainable fears) whose relation to significant life situations they may not understand or even suspect. In treating such clients, the crisis therapist generally finds it fruitful to follow initial inquiries with a review of the various aspects of the client's recent life experience (e.g., work, family, social and sexual relation).

In conducting such a review, analogous to the physician's "sys-

tems review," the therapist is particularly interested in learning of
life changes or events which may be temporally related to the
client's presenting complaints or "symptoms." Generally, this
review will uncover a significant problem or concern with which
the client has been struggling and which may be designated as the
problem-focus for intervention. The case examples[1] to follow illustrate how this "systems review" approach may be utilized in efforts to delineate a problem-focus in crisis intervention.

> *Case* 1. Ms. F., a forty-year-old widow presented with symp-
> toms of anxiety and mild depression. She told the therapist
> that she wanted "some pills to calm [her] down." When
> asked why she was seeking treatment at the present time, she
> explained that her home had recently been burglarized for
> the fifth time in eighteen months. Her television, stereo, and
> radio had been stolen, and now, she complained, "there's just
> nothing left to do." Though distraught, Ms. F. was not im-
> mobilized by the loss and stated that she planned to buy an-
> other "cheap" television, take out renter's insurance, and seek
> help in making her apartment more secure.
>
> Sensing that Ms. F. was actually coping quite well with her
> losses and suspecting that other factors might well be related
> to her anxiety and depression, the therapist proceeded to re-
> view with her the significant aspects of her recent life. This
> review revealed that Ms. F. had been steadily and happily em-
> ployed in the same job for many years, that she had a few
> close friends who were very supportive, and that she had had
> no romantic or sexual involvement for several years. The unex-
> pected loss of her husband had occurred many years earlier
> and seemed of little present concern to the client.
>
> When questioned about family relationships, however, Ms.
> F. burst into tears, exclaiming, "I love my children but they
> don't treat me right." She went on to explain that her rela-
> tionship with three grown children had been deteriorating in
> recent weeks. She told the therapist that all three were having
> problems of their own and were becoming increasingly de-
> pendent upon her, both emotionally and financially. She

1. Certain aspects of these actual cases have been altered to assure anonymity
and preserve the client's right to confidentiality.

added that she now even suspected that friends of one of her children might have been responsible for the burglaries.

Subsequently, Ms. F. and the therapist agreed that the intervention would focus on restoring a positive relationship between the client and her children. It was arranged to have all three of Ms. F.'s children present at the next treatment session, several days later.

Case 2. Ms. O., a twenty-one-year old unmarried mother of a four-year-old son. She arrived for her initial appointment complaining of debilitating anxiety, headaches, insomnia, and vague feelings that "something is going to happen to me." She told the therapist that she was seeking treatment at this time because her headaches, for which physicians had found no organic basis, were becoming unbearable. She explained that her symptoms had existed for many years, but had become persistent only in recent months. When asked if she could relate either the onset or the exacerbation of her symptoms to any significant events or life changes, Ms. O. replied that she could not.

Noting that Ms. O.'s admission forms indicated that she was an unmarried mother and recognizing that this is often a stressful role, the therapist began his "systems review" with an inquiry into the client's relationship with her son. Initially, Ms. O. was somewhat defensive and evasive, telling the therapist that although her child was born out of wedlock, she loved him very much and could see no reason for "dragging him into this."

Aware that he was touching upon a sensitive issue, the therapist persisted, gently but firmly, in exploring the mother-child relationship. He responded to Ms. O.'s defensiveness by explaining that raising a child alone was a difficult and stressful task and that her symptoms might be stress-related. Ms. O. became noticeably less defensive and told the therapist that she had been lucky in this regard: until just recently her child had been raised in a foster home.

Following this significant disclosure, it took only little further inquiry to determine that Ms. O.'s symptoms had become unbearable for the first time shortly after she had resumed custody of her son. Once the therapist suggested the likely connection between this event and the exacerbation of her symptoms, Ms. O. readily acknowledged that her foremost concern at present was not her symptoms but rather her growing feelings of guilt, frustration, and maternal inadequacy. Ultimately, this revelation led to an agreement that the intervention would focus on helping Ms. O. develop more effective parenting skills.

This "systems review" approach is useful not only in delineating the problem-focus, but also in assessing the extent to which each of the client's life "systems" relates to the identified problem(s). Not infrequently, the crisis therapist finds a problem-focus in one "system" but contributing or mitigating factors in other "systems." In planning an effective intervention, the therapist must carefully consider *all* of the clients' life "systems." An addendum to the case of Ms. O. illustrates this point:

Although Ms. O.'s relationship to her son was regarded as the problem-focus for intervention, it was also learned that her difficulties with him were aggravated by the fact that she was unemployed and had no close friends or relatives living nearby. Living on a very limited income and having no social or familial support network, Ms. O. was forced to spend virtually every waking hour with her son. Naturally this observation had clear implications for the planning of an appropriate intervention.

Evaluation

As has been observed in this volume, psychiatric diagnosis is often regarded as unessential, if not counterproductive, in crisis intervention. This is not to say, however, that the application of crisis intervention techniques is advocated in the absence of careful evaluation of the client. Indeed, while crisis therapists rarely bother with formal diagnostic classification, they invariably endeavor to evaluate carefully, if quickly, the client and his current life situation.

While identified here for convenience as the second stage of crisis intervention, evaluation actually begins the moment client and therapist meet, and continues, to some degree, throughout treatment. The therapist's initial observations and efforts at delineating a problem-focus are, in themselves, significant aspects of evaluation. Generally, however, adequate evaluation in crisis intervention requires that information derived through these measures be supplemented by additional data regarding the client's functioning and life situation. Prior to planning and implementing specific interventions, the crisis therapist should extend the evaluation process in at least the following directions:

1. Basic demographic data

In all cases, the crisis therapist should be aware of demographic data such as the client's age, marital and familial status, place of residence, education, and occupation. Such basic data serve two important functions. First, they provide the therapist with early (however tentative) insights into the client's difficulties. Second, they offer a basis for more extensive inquiry into various aspects of the client's functioning and life situation. The case of Ms. O., described earlier, illustrates the use of such data in this regard.

Some crisis therapists elicit basic demographic data through direct questioning of the client. Often, however, the therapist prefers to save valuable time and effort by obtaining the data from backgrounding documents such as forms filled out by the client or a clerical worker prior to the initial interview.

2. Brief treatment history

While the emphasis in crisis intervention is on the "here and now," most crisis therapists find it helpful, if not essential, to have at least some idea of the client's previous treatment experience. Clients with many earlier psychiatric contacts need not be ruled out as suitable candidates for crisis intervention, but should be approached with some caution. Such clients may have valid reasons for frequently seeking psychiatric help. On the other hand, they may be "doctor shoppers" who seek help often but rarely make any real commitment to treatment. In assessing the client with multiple prior psychiatric contacts, the crisis therapist should carefully inquire as to the circumstances surrounding the initiation and termination of such contacts before committing further time and resources to the client.

In addition to ascertaining treatment history, it is vital that the crisis therapist determine whether the client is already in ongoing treatment elsewhere. In general, the therapist should avoid establishing a treatment contract with clients currently under the care of other psychiatric clinicians or agencies. If a client is insistent and clearly wishes to change therapists, the crisis clinician should take pains to understand the client's motives and, as a rule, consult with the other therapist or agency before making any commitment to the client.

3. Accessibility to evaluation

In every case the crisis therapist must make an initial determination as to whether the client's condition allows for immediate, accurate evaluation. While the therapist will find most clients accessible to evaluation, there are some important exceptions. For example, clients who are intoxicated or heavily under the influence of sedative, tranquilizing, or psychedelic drugs generally cannot be accurately evaluated. Likewise, clients who are extremely agitated or suffering from overwhelming anxiety are often inaccessible at the time they first present themselves for treatment. The crisis therapist should have available a "detoxification" and/or short-stay inpatient facility to which these clients may be referred pending accessibility to evaluation.

4. *Psychological functioning*

While a full-scale, formal mental status examination is rarely included in crisis intervention, the therapist should carefully observe and evaluate at least the following aspects of the client's psychological functioning:

A. *Appearance and behavior* The crisis therapist should pay close attention to the client's mode of dress, physical characteristics, postures, facial expressions, motor activity, and manner of relating. These aspects of the client's appearance and behavior frequently help the therapist to understand and formulate an approach to the client's problems. For example, a neatly dressed, trim, handsome young man who relates warmly and openly but complains that he is rejected by women will most certainly require an intervention different from that offered an unkempt, overweight, somewhat homely and hostile man with the same problem.

B. *Speech* Psychotherapy of any kind is a verbal endeavor. Indeed, it has often been referred to as the "talking treatment" or, more optimistically, the "talking cure." Crisis intervention is no exception. Thus, an essential aspect of evaluation is an assessment of the way in which the client expresses himself verbally. The client who cannot or will not speak relatively openly and coherently may not be a suitable candidate for any kind of psychotherapy, particularly one such as crisis intervention, which moves so quickly and requires a high level of verbal interaction.

C. *Thought and perception* Crisis intervention, being a highly focused, fast-paced, and reality-oriented treatment modality, generally requires that the client be reasonably capable of clear, organized thinking, and relatively realistic perception. Thus, in evaluating the client's psychological functioning, the crisis therapist should always be alert to indications of intellectual retardation, formal thought disorder, delusions, and hallucinations. Cases in which the client's thinking and/or perception is grossly impaired by one or more of these or other features may not be appropriate for crisis intervention.

D. *Affect* The crisis therapist should observe carefully the client's mood and emotional responsiveness. In particular, the therapist should be alert to evidence of disturbances of affect such as depression, anxiety, apathy, or inappropriateness. The client may be questioned as to his feelings, but the therapist should also look to postures, facial expressions, and motor activity for clues.

The client whose affect is grossly inappropriate may be suffering from serious thought disorder. A careful effort should be made to assess the form and content of such a client's thinking prior to planning any intervention. The client who appears apathetic (i.e., displays inadequate affect) may also be suffering from thought disorder, may be "emotionally exhausted," or may simply be unmotivated. In any event, the therapist should determine the cause of the client's apathy before making any start at intervention.

As was observed earlier, the extremely anxious client may not be accessible to evaluation. Where the client is accessible, however, the therapist should note both the intensity and "type" of anxiety the client is experiencing. In crisis intervention it is particularly important to determine whether the client's anxiety is "normal" (i.e., based upon a realistic appraisal of threat or danger) or "neurotic" (i.e., out of proportion to any external threat or danger), and whether it is "specific" (i.e., elicited by a particular stimulus or set of circumstances) or "free-floating" (i.e., attached to no particular external stimulus). Given the realistic focus of crisis intervention, the therapist will generally find it less difficult to treat clients whose anxiety is "normal" or at least "specific."

In treating clients with severe "neurotic" or "free-floating" anxiety, the therapist may find the short-term use of anti-anxiety medications (the so-called "minor tranquilizers") a useful adjunct to crisis intervention. *Within reasonable limits,* however, anxiety may serve as a powerful force in motivating the client toward needed change. The indiscriminate use of tranquilizers may provide temporary symptom relief that leads clients to feel that their problems have been solved, thus reducing greatly their motivation for change and the likelihood that they may benefit from crisis intervention.

The depressed client presents perhaps the most serious challenge to the crisis therapist's clinical skills. In dealing with all depressed clients, the therapist must carefully assess 1. the suicidal risk; and 2. whether the client's depression is reactive (i.e., in response to an identifiable loss or personal setback).

In general, it is not inappropriate for the therapist to ask the client directly, "Have you had any thoughts of hurting or killing yourself?" Even if the client denies suicidal ideation or intent, however, the therapist should remain alert to both verbal and non-verbal clues indicative of suicidal feelings. If the client does appear to present a suicidal risk (i.e., has a plan, means, and opportunity for taking his own life), naturally the foremost concern for intervention will be the prevention of self-destructive behavior. When the danger of suicide seems imminent, the therapist should take immediate steps to arrange some sort of protective care for the client.

The client who presents a picture of reactive depression of mild-to-moderate intensity may respond well to crisis intervention. Once the nature and meaning of the loss or setback is understood, intervention may be directed toward enabling the client to cope more effectively. Depression that is especially severe and/or has no apparent roots in loss or setback, however, may not respond well to crisis intervention and is sometimes better handled with appropriate medical intervention (e.g., anti-depressant medications).

5. Pre-crisis adjustment

Since a major goal of crisis intervention is to restore the client to at least his pre-crisis level of functioning, the therapist must have some notion of the client's previous adjustment. Thus, briefly at least, the therapist must depart from the "here and now" emphasis and seek a fair amount of historical data regarding the client's general level of functioning.

There are several ways in which such data may be obtained. The first, of course, is through direct inquiry of the client. Specifically, the therapist might inquire as to how the client has perceived and dealt with earlier life "crises." Exploration of the client's responses to normal developmental "crises" (e.g., entering and leaving school, leaving home, marriage, parenthood) is often fruitful in ascertaining prior patterns of adjustment. Naturally, the client's work and school history, treatment history, family relationships, and experience with alcohol, drugs, and crime will also provide helpful clues.

As a second avenue to such data, the therapist may wish to make direct inquiries of family members, friends, employers, teachers, former therapists, and others who know the client and can comment on his previous functioning. Such inquiries, of course, should be made only with the client's informed and prior consent.

6. Motivation

While important in all forms of psychotherapy, client motivation is a particularly significant issue in crisis intervention. The short-term nature of this modality demands the client's active participation and precludes extensive working-through of resistance. As has been indicated earlier in this volume, there is much empirical evidence to suggest that positive client motivation is related significantly to successful outcome in crisis intervention.

Assessment of motivation may take a number of forms. The therapist will learn much about a client's motivation by exploring the ways in which he has attempted to master or cope with his problems before seeking help. The client who has already attempted actively to cope with his problems is likely to be more motivated than the client who has reacted passively and given little thought to possible adaptive courses of action. Likewise, the client who seeks professional help of his own accord is often more highly motivated than the client who seeks help only after being pressured by others.

In dealing with families, the crisis therapist frequently can assess motivation in much these same ways. In addition, however, the therapist should consider the extent to which family members are united in the decision to seek outside help. Where there is significant disagreement among family members, overall motivation may be questionable. The therapist should be aware that, in such cases, reluctant family members may interfere with or even sabotage the intervention.

Naturally, each case is unique, and there are no acid tests of client motivation. Generally, though, by the end of the first interview, the careful crisis therapist will have gathered enough data to determine whether the client's (or family's) motivation is sufficient to make additional sessions worthwhile. Where motivation is questionable or apparently lacking, the therapist should seriously consider whether the investment of additional time and resources is justified. Often, in such cases, it is appropriate for the therapist to share his concerns about motivation with the client, suggesting that the client take time to reconsider the request for treatment. The client may then call for another appointment, if and when he feels capable of making the kind of commitment required by crisis intervention.

Contracting

Once a problem-focus has been identified and agreed upon and the therapist is satisfied that the client may benefit from crisis intervention, a treatment contract should be negotiated. In crisis intervention the contract is especially important because it structures the limited time available, reinforces the time-limited and highly focused nature of the treatment, and offers the client a realistic idea of what to expect.

The contract in crisis intervention may be written or verbal. It should be understandable to the client and as explicit as possible. Generally, the contract should include *at least* the following categories of specification:

1. *The problem-focus*

The problem(s) to be dealt with in the intervention should be clearly stated. Vague statements, such as "We will work on your problems at school," should be avoided. Every effort should be made to state the problem(s) in terms of specific goals to be accomplished, such as "We will work toward developing a more realistic study schedule."

2. *Time limits*

The outside limits of the intervention should be made explicit in terms of available interview hours, number of sessions, or both. Generally, no minimum limits should be set. Scheduling of sessions may be left negotiable, but a limit in number of weeks should be set. If the client is to receive special consideration (such as evening or weekend appointments) this should also be spelled out.

3. Inclusion of others

An agreement should be reached as to which, if any, of the client's relatives or friends may be included in the treatment sessions. Client and therapist should agree also as to whom the therapist may contact in seeking or exchanging information about the client.

4. Responsibilities

The responsibilities of both client and therapist should be specified. The client will keep appointments; work actively with the therapist to explore his problems honestly and openly; strive to develop and implement realistic, adaptive solutions; and avoid behavior that creates, maintains, or exacerbates problems. The therapist will keep appointments; listen to the client; maintain confidentiality; and work actively with the client to help him understand his problems and resources, see the consequences of his behavior, become aware of alternatives, and develop realistic solutions.

Intervening

While described here for convenience as a separate stage, intervention obviously occurs throughout crisis therapy. Delineation of a problem-focus, evaluation, and contracting are, in themselves, important interventions. The nature of additional interventions in crisis therapy, of course, will depend upon the problems, needs, and resources of the client as well as upon the clinical judgment, skills, and ingenuity of the therapist. What follows here is a brief consideration of some, but by no means all, of the more common intervention tactics employed by crisis therapists.

1. Listening

Listening is so fundamental to effective psychotherapy that most clinicians take it for granted and would hesitate to describe it as a "tactic." Yet in discussing crisis intervention, in which such a high premium is placed upon therapist activity and aggressiveness, there is often a need to remind even experienced clinicians of the great value of listening.

Since time is so limited, the crisis therapist must actively direct the course of treatment, strive to maintain the problem-focus, and endeavor to minimize unnecessary digression. At all times, however, the therapist must be sensitive to the client's needs for expression and catharsis, allowing him adequate leeway to verbalize his emotional reactions, intellectual understanding of the problems, and ideas regarding their solution. Indeed, with clients who are passive or reluctant to express feelings and offer ideas, the therapist must not only listen but actively encourage verbalization.

2. Utilizing interpersonal resources

Rarely does a client experience problems alone. Almost invariably, others close to the client are affected, if not directly involved. Indeed, more often than not, clients present problems that are rooted, at least in part, in one or more of their significant interpersonal relationships.

This being so, the crisis therapist will seek to utilize the input, influence, and encouragement of significant others in the client's behalf, and will in addition encourage the client to seek personally and utilize the help of others. Where appropriate and feasible, certain of the client's closest friends and/or family members should be included in the treatment process.

3. *Utilizing institutional resources*

Not infrequently a client will require services and/or information the therapist is not equipped to provide. For example, clients may require educational counseling, financial assistance, job placement, birth control information, legal advice, medical treatment, or child care services. In such cases, referral to appropriate institutional resources in the community may be an important aspect of crisis intervention.

4. *Advocacy*

Related to the utilization of interpersonal and institutional resources is client advocacy. Many client problems are directly related to the failure of certain individuals or institutions to respond appropriately to their legitimate needs. To avoid fostering dependence, crisis therapists ordinarily encourage such clients to turn to alternative resources or to develop more effective ways of approaching the unresponsive parties. In some cases, however, the client's needs are not only legitimate but urgent and the therapist may find it necessary to assume, temporarily, the role of advocate, intervening personally with the unresponsive individual or institution in the client's behalf.

5. *Confrontation*

Frequently and often unknowingly, clients play a significant role in creating and maintaining their own problems. Often they persist in self-defeating behavior, over-utilize defense mechanisms to the point where they are maladaptive, and/or cling to unrealistic attitudes or beliefs that preclude effective coping. Consider, for example, the husband who works at two full-time jobs, drinks heavily, and spends weekends hunting and fishing with the boys, and yet cannot understand why his wife is ready to leave him;

the young working woman who is financially independent but
continues to live at home and complains that her parents are
"trying to run" her life; or the parents who have never said *no* to
their teen-age son and yet "wonder" why he presents a behavior
problem at home and school.

In long-term psychotherapy, the therapist may work in subtle
ways to help clients understand how they contribute to their own
problems. In crisis intervention, however, time is too precious for
such subtlety, and the therapist must often move quickly to confront clients with maladaptive aspects of their behavior and/or
attitudes. Pointed questioning and interpretation may be sufficient
for this purpose. If necessary, however, the therapist should not
be reluctant to comment directly and critically upon the client's
maladaptive, self-defeating, or unrealistic ways. In this regard, crisis
therapists often find it useful to predict for clients the ultimate
(sometimes dire) consequences of persisting in certain maladaptive behaviors or attitudes.

6. *Giving information*

The maladaptive behavior of many clients appears based, at least
in part, on some form of misinformation. Consider, for example,
the young unmarried woman who is overwhelmed at learning that
she is pregnant, knows that she cannot care adequately for a child
in the near future, wishes an abortion but will not consider one because she has heard that an abortion "leaves you sterile"; the teen-
ager who, having succumbed to the homosexual advances of an
older man, believes that he now "must be gay"; or the college
student who, having done only average work in one science course,
is considering suicide because now she will "never get into medical school."

In any case in which the client is acting on misinformation or
faulty assumptions, the crisis therapist often can be quite helpful
simply by providing factual information. The therapist is usually

perceived as a knowledgeable, authoritative source; hence there is usually no need for lengthy, detailed, or scientific explanations. The therapist may, however, wish to offer the client documentation or referral to a corroborating source of information, where such is available and appropriate.

7. Exploring alternative coping mechanisms

Many clients approach treatment with the explanation that they have tried "everything" in their struggle to cope with or resolve their problems. Only rarely, however, is this actually so: the client has usually overlooked or prematurely discarded some potentially adaptive coping mechanisms. A primary task in every intervention is enabling the client to be aware of and to consider carefully all reasonable alternative coping mechanisms.

Since it is basic to evaluation in crisis intervention, exploration of the steps the client has already taken to cope with or resolve his difficulties is perhaps the most sensible way to begin this task. In considering the client's recent, apparently unsuccessful coping efforts, the crisis therapist will seek to understand not only what attempts have been made but also why these attempts have failed. Not infrequently, this approach reveals that certain coping mechanisms that have apparently failed may, with appropriate modification and/or greater client effort, turn out to be quite effective.

In addition to exploring recent coping efforts, the therapist may also find it helpful to consider strategies that the client has utilized successfully in dealing with past problems. Most clients have experienced at least some measure of success in past coping efforts. With encouragement and reinforcement, many of them may be able to apply such experience to their current situation.

If exploration of recent and past coping efforts fails to yield potentially viable coping strategies, the client must be encouraged to think of and verbalize as many new alternative strategies as possible. The therapist may then focus upon, clarify, and reinforce those mechanisms that seem most promising. In some cases, on the other hand, the therapist will find it necessary to suggest alternatives to the client. As is indicated in the following section, the therapist should exercise caution in making direct suggestions or giving advice to clients.

8. *Advice and suggestion*

Though frowned upon by many traditional psychotherapists, the use of advice and suggestion is sometimes both appropriate and necessary in crisis intervention; but the therapist should be aware of the potential risks involved.

Some clients will take the advice and "run with it," terminating treatment prematurely in the belief that they have been given "the answer" to their problems. Others will resist advice and may respond with, "I've done that already and it doesn't work." Worst of all, still other clients may take the therapist's suggestions only to find that they are inappropriate, unworkable, or even damaging. Given these risks, the crisis therapist would do well to use advice and suggestion sparingly and cautiously with all clients, and probably not at all with clients who are particularly resistant or are seeking easy, pat answers to complex problems.

9. *Behavioral task assignment*

Related to, yet distinct from, advice and suggestion is the assignment of behavioral tasks, in which the crisis therapist directs the client to perform certain specific behaviors outside of treatment sessions. These tasks or behavioral prescriptions, often designated as "homework," are not viewed as "solutions" but rather as opportunities for the client to practice particular coping skills that may ultimately help him in solving his problems.

For example: the shy, timid young woman who complains that

she is easily intimidated by male subordinates at work may be directed to practice certain assertive behaviors in her dealings with other men between treatment sessions. Or the parents of an unruly adolescent may be instructed to practice saying *no* to, and not backing down in the face of, certain of his unreasonable demands. In some cases the therapist will want to supplement task assignment with some form of "behavioral rehearsal," providing the client an opportunity to practice the tasks with the therapist during the session in which they are assigned.

Like advice and suggestion, task assignment has its risks and should be used judiciously. The client should always be warned of possible adverse consequences, prepared to deal with them, and advised that assigned tasks are for practice in developing certain coping skills and should not be viewed as direct solutions to problems.

Termination

Since the duration of crisis intervention is made explicit to the client early in treatment, termination should come as no surprise. This does not mean, however, that termination in crisis intervention is invariably an easy task requiring little consideration or effort. The termination of any meaningful relationship may be expected to evoke strong sentiments. Though brief and highly focused, the relationship between crisis therapist and client is generally no exception.

Typically, the therapist prepares the client for termination by carefully stating explicit time limits early in treatment and by devoting portions of the last few sessions to a discussion of this issue. The therapist who utilizes this approach, however, must be careful to limit such discussion in early sessions lest termination become the major treatment issue. Reactions to termination vary from client to client and, for the most part, dictate the specific ways in which the issue is ultimately handled. To illustrate:

Some clients view termination with a sense of accomplishment and independence. Their reactions indicate that they feel benefited by the intervention and optimistic regarding their coping capacities. With these clients, the therapist need do little more than reinforce the client's positive feelings, wish them the best, and casually note that further help is available should the need for it arise.

Some clients regard termination as a serious threat to their needs and develop acute feelings of sadness, fear, or even dread. Not infrequently, such clients will, consciously or unconsciously, seek to prolong the intervention by raising new problems or regressing in their behavior at the last minute. When this occurs, the crisis therapist does well to focus attention on the client's underlying feelings rather than the newly raised problems or regressive behavior.

First of all, the therapist should seek to understand the client's feelings and relate them verbally to the client's efforts to prolong treatment. Then, the therapist may openly empathize with the client (sharing some of his own emotional reactions to termination), accentuate the accomplishments of the intervention, express appropriate optimism regarding the client's current coping abilities, schedule a follow-up visit some months in the future, or (if warranted) offer to refer the client to another therapist or agency for additional help. In all cases, however, the therapist should enforce the treatment contract and endeavor to achieve termination as scheduled.

Some clients react to termination with no apparent concern, denying that they have any particular feelings about ending treatment. In dealing with such clients, the crisis therapist should not force the issue, but should, on the other hand, resist the temptation to allow the client to leave treatment without any real consideration of termination-related sentiments. The brevity of crisis intervention precludes extensive efforts to facilitate such consideration, but ordinarily the therapist can act quickly to encourage expression and consideration of feelings around termination. For example, the therapist may reveal to the client some of his own feelings about termination and wonder aloud whether the client is "feeling the same way"—or taking a more direct tact, simply ask the client, "How are you feeling about ending treatment?"

Perhaps most difficult of all for the crisis therapist are those cases in which the client terminates prematurely and without notice. When such a situation occurs, the therapist should actively endeavor to re-establish contact with the client to discover why he has left treatment.

When a client terminates early in treatment or even after only a single session, it may be that he feels sufficiently benefited or that his life situation has taken an unexpected turn for the better. If either of these is the case, the therapist need only point out to him that further help is available if and when the need should arise. Occasionally, however, a client will terminate early and without notice simply to "test" the therapist's concern or commitment. A brief contact, such as suggested above, is usually enough to reassure the client and facilitate his return to treatment.

When a client fails to return for scheduled visits toward the end of treatment, this may be his way of avoiding the issue of termination. In such cases also, the therapist should contact the client, inquiring about his reasons for leaving treatment, encouraging at least some discussion of termination-related sentiments, and offering to complete the treatment contract if the client so desires.

Follow-up

Regardless of how a client has terminated, the crisis therapist should make an effort to ascertain the client's condition and progress sometime after treatment is concluded. Follow-up—usually in the form of a phone call a month or two following termination—serves important evaluative, educational, and clinical functions.

In terms of evaluation, follow-up offers at least a minimal assessment of the efficacy of the intervention. Educationally, it provides feedback helpful to therapists in developing or sharpening their crisis intervention skills. Clinically, it enables the therapist to reinforce especially significant aspects of the intervention, discover whether referrals have been followed through, and re-evaluate the client's need for additional treatment or referral.

Bibliography

Ancell, H. Participation of marital partners in the treatment of patients in a crisis agency. Doctoral dissertation, University of Southern California, 1972. University Microfilms 72–25994.

Argles, P., and Mackenzie, M. Crisis intervention with a multiproblem family: a case study. *Journal of Child Psychology and Psychiatry*, 1970, 11, 187–95.

Atkins, M., Fischer, M., Prater, G., Winget, C., and Zaleski, J. Brief treatment of homosexual patients. *Comprehensive Psychiatry*, 1976, 17, 115–24.

Bartolucci, G., and Drayer, C. S. An overview of crisis intervention in the emergency rooms of general hospitals. *American Journal of Psychiatry*, 1973, 130, 953–60.

Beigel, A., and Levenson, A. I. *The community mental health center*. New York: Basic Books, 1972.

Berlin, I. Crisis intervention and short-term therapy: an approach in a child-psychiatric clinic. *Journal of Child Psychiatry*, 1970, 9, 595–606.

Bloom, B. L. Definitional aspects of the crisis concept. *Journal of Consulting Psychology*, 1963, 27, 498–502.

Bonstedt, T. Crisis intervention or early access brief therapy? *Diseases of the Nervous System*, 1970, 783–87.

Burgess, A., and Holmstrom, L. Rape trauma syndrome. *American Journal of Psychiatry*, 1974, 131, 981–86.

Butcher, J. N., and Maudal, G. R. Crisis intervention. In I. B.

Weiner, ed., *Clinical methods in psychology*. New York: Wiley, 1976.

Caplan, G. Patterns of parent response to the crisis of premature birth. *Psychiatry*, 1960, 23, 365–74.

————. *Principles of preventive psychiatry*. New York: Basic Books, 1964.

Caplan, G., ed. *The prevention of mental disorders in children*. New York: Basic Books, 1961.

Chandler, H. M. Family crisis intervention. *Journal of the National Medical Association*, 1972, 64, 211–16, and 224.

Christ, J. The adolescent crisis syndrome: its clinical significance in the outpatient service. *Psychiatric Forum*, 1972, 3, 25–34.

Clark, S. C., and Rootman, I. Street-level drug crisis intervention. *Drug Forum*, 1974, 3, 239-47.

Cowan, B., Currie, M., Krol, R., and Richardson, J. Holding unwilling clients in treatment. *Social Casework*, 1969, 50, 146–51.

Crum, R. S. Counseling rape victims. *Journal of Pastoral Care*, 1974, 28, 112–21.

Darbonne, A. R. Crisis: a review of theory, practice and research. *Psychotherapy: Theory, Research and Practice*, 1967, 4, 49–56.

Decker, J. B., and Stubblebine, J. M. Crisis intervention and prevention of psychiatric disability: a follow-up study. *American Journal of Psychiatry*, 1972, 129, 725–29.

Duckworth, G. L. A project in crisis intervention. *Social Casework*, 1967, 48, 227–31.

Eastham, K., Coates, D., and Allodi, F. The concept of crisis. *Canadian Psychiatric Association Journal*, 1970, 15, 463–71.

Eisler, R. M., and Hersen, M. Behavioral techniques in family-oriented crisis intervention. *Archives of General Psychiatry*, 1973, 28, 111-16.

Erikson, E. H. *Childhood and society*. New York: Norton, 1950.

————. Identity and the life cycle. *Psychological Issues Monograph*, 1959, 1, no. 1.

Ewalt, P. L. The crisis-treatment approach in a child guidance clinic. *Social Casework*, 1973, 54, 406–11.

Ewalt, P. L., and Cohen, M. Planning a crisis treatment program to enhance professional growth. Paper presented at the annual meeting of the Association of Psychiatric Services for Children, Beverly Hills, Calif., November 1971.

Ewing, C. P. Family crisis intervention and traditional child guidance: a comparison of outcome and factors related to success in treatment. Doctoral dissertation, Cornell University, 1975.

————. Evaluating family crisis intervention. Paper presented at the annual meeting of the American Association of Psychiatric Services for Children, San Francisco, November 1976.

Fallon, C. Providing relevant brief service to couples in marital crises. *American Journal of Orthopsychiatry*, 1973, 43, 235–36.

Flomenhaft, K., and Langsley, D. G. After the crisis. *Mental Hygiene*, 1971, 55, 473–77.

Fox, S. S., and Scherl, D. J. Crisis intervention with rape victims. *Social Work*, 1972, 17, 37–42.

Frank, J. Problems of controls in psychotherapy. In E. A. Rubenstein and M. B. Parloff, eds., *Research in psychotherapy. Vol. I.* Washington, D.C.: American Psychological Association, 1962.

Galdston, R., and Hughes, M. C. Pediatric hospitalization as crisis intervention. *American Journal of Psychiatry*, 1972, 129, 721–25.

Golden, L. H., Golden, N. P., and Dibiase, J. Crisis intervention for cardiac outpatients. *Medical Insight*, 1972, 4, 18–23.

Goldsmith, W., and Zeitlin, M. Crisis therapy for disaster victims. *Exchange*, 1973, 1, 3–7.

Gottschalk, L. A., Fox, R. A., and Bates, D. E. A study of prediction and outcome in a mental health crisis clinic. *American Journal of Psychiatry*, 1973, 130, 1107–11.

Halpern, H. Crisis theory: a definitional study. *Community Mental Health Journal*, 1973, 9, 342–49.

Hankoff, L. D., Mischorr, M. T., Tomlinson, K. E., and Joyce, S. A. A program of crisis intervention in the emergency medical setting. *American Journal of Psychiatry*, 1974, 131, 47–50.

Helig, S. M., Farberow, N. L., Litman, R. E., and Schneidman, E. S. The role of non-professional volunteers in a suicide prevention center. *Community Mental Health Journal*, 1968, 4, 287–95.

Hitchcock, J. M. Crisis intervention: the pebble in the pool. *American Journal of Nursing*, 1973, 73, 1388–90.

Hoffman, D. L., and Remmel, M. L. Uncovering the precipitant in crisis intervention. *Social Casework*, 1975, 56, 259–67.

Jacobson, G. F. Crisis theory and treatment strategy: some sociocultural and psychodynamic considerations. *Journal of Nervous and Mental Diseases*, 1965, 141, 209–18.

Jacobson, G. F.   Some psychoanalytic considerations regarding crisis therapy. *Psychoanalytic Review*, 1967, 54, 93–98.

Jaffe, D. T.   The repression and support of psychedelic experience. In G. A. Specter and W. L. Claiborn, eds., *Crisis intervention.* New York: Behavioral Publications, 1973.

Kaffman, M.   Short-term family therapy. *Family Process*, 1963, 2. Reprinted in H. J. Parad, ed., *Crisis intervention: Selected readings.* New York: FSAA, 1965, 202–19.

Kaplan, D. M.   Observations on crisis theory and practice. *Social Casework*, 1968, 49, 151–55.

Kaplan, D. M., and Mason, E. A.   Maternal reactions to premature birth viewed as an acute emotional disorder. *American Journal of Orthopsychiatry*, 1960, 30, 539–52.

Kardener, S. H.   A methodologic approach to crisis therapy. *American Journal of Psychotherapy*, 1975, 29, 4–13.

Kiresuk, T. J., and Sherman, R. E.   Goal attainment scaling: A general method for evaluating comprehensive community mental health programs. *Community Mental Health Journal*, 1968, 4, 443–53.

Kissel, S.   Mothers and therapists evaluate long-term and short-term child therapy. *Journal of Clinical Psychology*, 1974, 30, 296-99.

Klein, D. C., and Lindemann, E.   Preventive intervention in individual and family crisis situations. In G. Caplan, ed., *The prevention of mental disorders in children.* New York: Basic Books, 1961.

Lang, J.   Planned short-term treatment in a family agency. *Social Casework*, 1974, 55, 369–74.

Langsley, D. G.   Crisis intervention. *American Journal of Psychiatry*, 1972, 129, 734–36.

Langsley, D. G., and Kaplan, D.   *The treatment of families in crisis.* New York: Grune and Stratton, 1968.

Langsley, D. G., Pittman, F. S., Machotka, P., and Flomenhaft, K. Family crisis therapy: results and implications. *Family Process*, 1968, 7, 145–58.

Lau, H., and Cooper, S.   A night in crisis. *Psychiatry*, 1973, 36, 23–36.

LaVietes, R. L.   Crisis intervention for ghetto children: contraindications and alternative considerations. *American Journal of Orthopsychiatry*, 1974, 44, 720–27.

Lester, D., and Brockoff, G. W., eds.   *Crisis intervention and counseling by telephone.* Springfield, Ill.: Charles C Thomas, 1973.

Lindemann, E. Symptomatology and management of acute grief. *American Journal of Psychiatry*, 1944, 101, 141–48.

Mackenzie, K., and Bruce, D. A comprehensive community drug center. *Hospital and Community Psychiatry*, 1972, 23, 318–21.

McColskey, A. S. Models of crisis intervention: the crisis counseling model. In G. A. Specter and W. L. Claiborn, eds., *Crisis intervention*. New York: Behavioral Publications, 1973.

McCombie, S. L., Bassuk, E., Savitz, R., and Pell, S. Development of a medical center rape crisis intervention program. *American Journal of Psychiatry*, 1976, 133, 418–21.

McGee, R. K. *Crisis intervention in the community.* Baltimore: University Park Press, 1974.

McGee, T. F. Some basic considerations in crisis intervention. *Community Mental Health Journal*, 1968, 4, 319–25.

Meltzoff, J., and Kornreich, M. *Research in psychotherapy*. New York: Atherton, 1970.

Nelson, Z. P., and Mowry, D. D. Contracting in crisis intervention. *Community Mental Health Journal*, 1976, 12, 37–43.

Newman, M. B., and San Martino, M. Therapeutic intervention in a community child psychiatric clinic. *Journal of Child Psychiatry*, 1969, 8, 692-710.

Nigro, S. A psychiatrist's experiences in general practice in a hospital emergency room. *Journal of the American Medical Association*, 1970, 214, 1657–68.

Parad, H. J., ed. *Crisis intervention: Selected readings.* New York: FSAA, 1965.

Parad, H. J., and Caplan, G. A framework for studying families in crisis. *Journal of Social Work*, 1960, 5, 3–15.

Parad, H. J., and Parad, L. G. A study of crisis-oriented planned short-term treatment: part one. *Social Casework*, 1968, 49, 346–55.

Parad, L. G., and Parad, H. J. A study of crisis-oriented planned short-term treatment: part two. *Social Casework*, 1968, 49, 418–26.

Pasewark, R. A., and Albers, D. A. Crisis intervention: theory in search of a program. *Social Work*, 1972, 17, 70–77.

Patrick, J. D., and Wander, R. S. Treatment of the adolescent crisis patient. *Psychotherapy: Theory, Research and Practice*, 1974, 11, 246–49.

Patterson, V., and O'Sullivan, M. Three perspectives on brief psychotherapy. *American Journal of Psychotherapy*, 1974, 28, 265–77.

Porter, R. A.   Crisis intervention and social work models. *Community Mental Health Journal*, 1966, 2, 13–21.

Rapoport, L.   The state of crisis: some theoretical considerations. *Social Service Review*, 1962, 36. Reprinted in H. J. Parad, ed., *Crisis intervention: Selected readings*. New York: FSAA, 1965, 22–31.

Rapoport, R. V.   Normal crisis, family structure and mental health. *Family Process*, 1963, 2, 68–80.

Reid, W. J., and Shyne, A. W.   *Brief and extended casework*. New York: Columbia University Press, 1969.

Rexford, E. N.   Some meanings of aggressive behavior in children. *Annals of the American Academy of Political Science*, 1959, 322, 10–18.

Rubinstein, D.   Rehospitalization versus family crisis intervention. *American Journal of Psychiatry*, 1972, 129, 715–720.

Sackman, H.   *Guidelines for developing community programs to assist and re-educate drinking drivers. Vol. I.* Springfield, Va.: NTIS, 1972.

Sadler, R.   Grandparents do count. *Challenge*, 1973, 16, 13.

Schwartz, S. L.   A review of crisis intervention programs. *Psychiatric Quarterly*, 1971, 45, 498–508.

Sebolt, N.   Crisis intervention and its demands on the crisis therapist. In G. A. Specter and W. L. Claiborn, eds., *Crisis intervention*. New York: Behavioral Publications, 1973.

Serrano, A. C., and Gibson, G.   Mental health services to the Mexican-American community in San Antonio, Texas. *American Journal of Public Health*, 1973, 63, 1055–57.

Shaw, R., Blumenfeld, H., and Senf, R.   A short-term treatment program in a child guidance clinic. *Social Work*, 1968, 13, 81–90.

Specter, G. A., and Claiborn, W. L.   *Crisis intervention*. New York: Behavioral Publications, 1973.

Stone, J. P.   Some teenagers are still having babies. *Psychiatric Opinion*, 1975, 12, 29–35.

Stratton, J. G.   Effects of crisis intervention counseling on predelinquent and misdemeanor juvenile offenders. *Juvenile Justice*, 1975, 26, 7–18.

Taplin, J. R.   Crisis theory: critique and reformulation. *Community Mental Health Journal*, 1971, 7, 13–24.

Ten Broeck, E. The extended family center. *Children Today*, 1974, 3, 2–6.

Waldfogel, S., and Gardner, G. E.   Intervention in crises as a method of primary prevention. In G. Caplan, ed., *The prevention of mental disorders in children*. New York: Basic Books, 1961.

Wales, E. Crisis intervention in clinical training. *Professional Psychology*, 1972, 3, 357–61.

Weinberger, G. Brief therapy with children and their parents. In H. H. Barten, ed., *Brief therapies*. New York: Behavioral Publications, 1971.

Weiss, S. D., and Kapp, R. A.   An interdisciplinary campus mental health program specializing in crisis intervention services. *Professional Psychology*, 1974, 5, 25–31.

Wellisch, D. K., and Gay, G. R.   The walking wounded: emergency psychiatric intervention in a heroin addict population. *Drug Forum*, 1972, 1, 137–44.

Werhan, C. F.   Crisis pastoral care to the families of critically ill patients in a general hospital. Doctoral dissertation, 1973. University Microfilms 73–23189.

Wolberg, L. Psychiatric technics in crisis therapy. *New York State Journal of Medicine*, 1972, 72, 1266–69.

Wolkon, G. H. Crisis theory, the application for treatment, and dependency. *Comprehensive Psychiatry*, 1972, 13, 459–64.

Index

Subjects

841-65

3 0081 016 037 990

SOUTHERN

JUL 24 1985

BOUND